Praise For Embracing the Wisdom of the Wood Snake

This is a delig[illegible] a journey of inne[illegible] al understanding [illegible] l wisdom is delive[illegible] and gently layered into deepe[illegible] no previous experience required. It goes beyond the usual linear nature of books that speak to a topic or tell a story. Rather this book invites you to be so much more than passive reader, It calls you forth into a soulful and creative exploration of your own story. It guides you in, invites you to consider who you are in relationship to both Self and to t the dynamically unfolding nature and story of Creation as a living field in 2025. There is room to make the material very much your own, You can choose to explore and move with the months, the seasons, the elements, the phases, or a mix of all of these, The book invites you first to a self-commitment and then to partake in a co-operative collaborative partnership into, playing, listening, learning, engaging, creating, releasing, letting go, emerging and re-emerging able to act with heart, with greater awareness and rooted self-acceptance in a world in need. -

— Ann B. aka Wild Soul. Wicklow, Ireland.

Rev. Deb is a true artist in everything she does, whether it's her artwork, Daoist medicine or writing. This book is no different; its poetic beauty inspires reflection on every page, encouraging readers to appreciate the beauty of life and seize opportunities in every moment. It offers a gentle, positive reflection not only on the energy of the Year of the Wooden Snake, but also on the deeper dynamics through various aspects, including the changing seasons. I learned something on every page, often re-reading sentences or paragraphs, in awe of how Deb's spiritual guidance is delivered through such artistry.

—Josh Barrow Acupuncturist.
Surrey. UK
www.justlifesbalance.co.uk

Each New Year brings opportunities to shift, grow and create. We often set intentions, make resolutions and envision hopeful outcomes at the beginning of each year. Yet somehow we lose that "start-up energy" as our life takes on predictable paths and soon it's just business as usual. With Rev Deb Connor's handbook Embracing the Wisdom of the Wood Snake you have a guide to help you work with the elements and energies of this Chinese Year of the Wood

Snake to facilitate real change, growth and creativity in your life. Rev Deb breaks down the year into helpful sections. Understanding the energies of each season she gives you practices to harness that energy and move with it. She even gives a month by month outline of more specific exercises to use for growth. I highly recommend this book. Keep it by your journal. Look at it often. It helps you remember the power of the elements, energies and your own consciousness to create the life you want.

— **Mebbie Jackson Sound healer, yoga teacher, Priestess. Knoxville TN USA. @heartpathwellness.org**

Deb is a shining light in a world that is craving that light. Her love and care for her fellow planet beings comes through in her art, writing and healing work. I have had the privilege of journeying with Deb. I have seen the joy she has for living and the inner work she has done that now allows her to bring more insights to all of us. You will find that Deb opens doorways that allow you to walk through to a greater awareness of self and others. Enjoy this book, it is written from the Heart, embrace its wisdom and it will touch your own Heart- deeply.

— Wendy Farmer Enneagram and Mindfulness Meditation Teacher. USA

A truly inspiring, thoughtfully written and beautifully illustrated book that invites readers to reflect and explore and thus cultivate and transform their own journey through the year of the wood snake. A helpful guide of suggested practices, with monthly themes that inspire connection with and living in tune with the seasons, nature, elements and energies. I would highly recommend this book to anyone, no matter where they are on their own personal journey.

—Julie McEgan Retiree, lover of Life. @juliemcegan

Wow! These illustrations make me want to journal... and I don't like writing!

— Ann Gordon Artist, print maker.
London. UK

This book is truly brilliant and everyone needs their own copy. Don't just buy your own get one for anyone you care about, they'll love you for it.

— Neil R Peck, Outdoor Adventurer,
Hound Dad & Lover of Life

Embracing the Wisdom of the Wood Snake

Shedding, Growing and Journaling through 2025

Rev Deb Connor

To my dearest friend Helen,
Enjoy shedding these skins.
Much love and many Blessings,
Rev Deb ♥
xxx

Embracing the Wisdom of the Wood Snake

ISBN : 978-1-0684202-0-7

Published by Spiritual Bookworm

Rev. Deb Connor

Email: deb@debconnor.com

CONTENT DISCLAIMER

MEDICAL DISCLAIMER

Contents

Foreword

Every once in a while someone comes along who makes a lasting impression on our life. I first met Rev Deb when she was just Deb. We were on a week-long retreat, purging our psyche of all negativities. Amongst the tears there was also laughter. There was always lots of laughter with Deb. She effortlessly made the mundane tolerable and the dull hilarious! When she invited me to write a foreword for her new book, my first reaction was quite simply;

"What has she created now?"

She literally explodes with knowledge, wisdom and enthusiasm in every possible way. An accomplished artist, interfaith reverend, creativity mentor, journal therapist, published author and now the creator of this journaling guide. Not just a journal guide I must add. This journaling companion is quite extraordinary. The profound knowledge of the Chinese Year, the etheric energy cycles, The Dao, and much more, is gently drip-fed to us as we flow with the text and allow the many amazing, empowering techniques to bring us into harmonious alignment with the prevailing frequencies of that moment. I am in awe of the depth of Rev Deb's research, her deep understanding of the elements; Wood, Fire, Earth, Metal and Water. She effortlessly marries the Daoist principles of the five elements to the energetics of the Year of the Snake and the prevailing element of 2025, that of Wood. What a genius concept this journaling companion is! It guides us through the changing energetic frequencies, gently offering ways we can surrender to the flow, rather than live in stressful resistance. Within its pages we find brilliant suggestions to inspire us to journal enthusiastically. We are offered deeply insightful questions that entice us to discover our inner self, and how we too, can activate our inner power. As we flow through this inspiring work, we connect gently with the essence that is Rev Deb. We feel safe in her nurturing guidance, we feel befriended by the revelations she has encouraged us to discover about ourselves. Every once in while someone comes along who makes a lasting impression on our life.

This Journaling companion is 'that someone'. Constantly by our side, it becomes an impactful and powerful guide through the days ahead.

Teresa Brown, *Cheltenham, UK. January 2025*

Teresa is recognized as a pioneer in her field, having begun teaching spiritual awareness in the early 1980's. The author of 'Becoming More Spiritual' and 'An Essential Guide to Ascension: Living in the Fifth Dimension'. Teresa is a registered Life Coach, Hypnotherapist, Reiki Master Healer & Teacher. To find out more visit: www.relaxand-progress.co.uk

Welcome to the Year of the Wood Snake

You are standing at the threshold of a year unlike any other, there has never been, up until now that is, a 2025. This is a year steeped in transformation, creativity and the potent strategic wisdom of the Wood Snake. This book is your companion for navigating the Year of the Yin Wood Snake in 2025, a guide to aligning with the energies of the seasons, the elements and the cosmos. It's an invitation to embark on a journey of self-discovery, creative exploration and intentional living, all while embracing the mysteries and opportunities that the Wood Snake year holds.

Why This Book?

The idea for this book was born from my own experience of working with the rhythms of nature, the wisdom of Daoist philosophy and the insights of Chinese astrology can offer. Over the years, I've found that aligning with these energies to be totally transformational. I've seen how understanding the elemental cycles and seasonal shifts can illuminate the

path, fuel creativity and bring clarity to the challenges and opportunities that life offers. This book is the culmination of that inspiration, a heartfelt offering for those who, like me, seek a deeper connection with themselves, the world around them and with Spirit. This book is for anyone who feels the pull to pause, reflect and create with intention.

How to Use This Book

This is more than a book; it's a companion, a journaling guide and a permission slip for your exploration. Within these pages, you'll find monthly themes, journal prompts, meditative practices, rituals and creative exercises designed to support you in aligning with the flow of the Yin Wood Snake year. Each section is crafted to help you to leverage the distinct energies of the seasons and their associated elements, making them tools for inspiration, growth and transformation.

Whether you're a seasoned creative, regular journal writer or a curious beginner, this book invites you to approach journaling and creativity in your own unique way. You can follow the month by month section, dive into the prompts that call to you (and perhaps some that you feel resistant to) or simply use this as a source of inspiration when you need a little guidance and clarity.

How can this book help and support you?

This book has been written with my Heartfelt love to:

- **Illuminate Your Path:** Understand the unique energies of 2025 and how they influence your journey.
- **Ignite Your Creativity:** Explore new ways of expressing yourself and uncovering your passions.
- **Deepen Your Connection:** Align with the rhythms of nature and your own inner wisdom.
- **Transform Your Challenges:** Use reflection and intention to turn obstacles into opportunities for growth.

Above all, this book is a reminder that your life is a creative act, one that unfolds moment by moment, choice by choice. The Year of the Yin Wood Snake is an opportunity to step into your life with awareness and intention, to grow, create and transform in ways that resonate deeply with who you are.

An Invitation

As you open this book, I invite you to approach it with curiosity and an open heart. Let it be a mirror, a map and a canvas. Use it to explore your inner world, to honour your journey and to align with the energies of a year that promises profound growth and transformation.

A word about repetition

You will find throughout this book that some explanations of energetics and seasons are repeated in different chapters of this book. There are two main reasons for this (1) some things are simply worth repeating, it helps with learning and knowledge retention and (2) in service to those readers, like myself, who don't always read from cover to cover, each chapter can be dipped into without necessarily reading this book from start to finish.

This is *your* year.

Let's begin the journey together.

Dancing with the Dao and the Cosmic Blueprint of Chinese Astrology

You stand at the edge of a vast forest... the air alive with possibilities, the rustling leaves whisper ancient truths, sunlight filters through the canopy like fragments of an untold story.

This is the essence of Daoist philosophy, a way of seeing the world not as a series of random events but as a seamless, interconnected dance of nature, humanity and the cosmos. Rooted in the Dao, frequently translated as "The Way" or "The Path", this ancient wisdom beckons you to pause, observe and align yourself with the rhythms of life.

On the 29th of January 2025 you step into the Year of the Yin Wood Snake, seasonal rhythms take on a unique pace and pulse. This year is not one of frenetic activity but of purposeful steady growth. It is a time for peeling back the layers of what no longer serves you, planting seeds of intention and nurturing them with care. The energies and

phases of this year are a map, guiding you toward transformation, creativity and, if you choose it, profound transformation and renewal.

The Dao: Living in the Flow

The Dao isn't a rulebook or a doctrine. It's the quiet force that underlies and connects everything, it joins the dots. Dao is the stars in the sky, rivers carving their way persistently and quietly through mountains. It's the way your heart races when you hear that song- the one that feels as though it was written only for you. And it's the mud on your wellies that has now spread itself halfway up the carpet on your stairs. The Dao is the rhythm of existence itself, a current that flows through all things, inviting you to move with it not fight against it.

Living in harmony with the Dao means recognising that life is not about rigid control it's about flow. Letting go of struggling upstream against the river's natural flow- which leads to exhaustion and frustration. Rather surrendering to the current, letting its energy carry you forward. The Dao reminds you to listen to the world, to adapt, and to trust that the path will reveal itself as you walk it.

Yin and Yang: The Eternal Balance

Our life unfolds in cycles at the heart of which is the cosmic dance of Yin and Yang. Yin: introspective, quiet and soft. The gentle pull of the moon on the ocean's tides. Yang: outward, bold and dynamic. The sun blazing at noon. Together they form the foundation of all existence, not in opposition to each other but as partners endlessly weaving the fabric of reality. In the alternating cycle of Yin and Yang years 2025 falls as a Yin year. The overall energy leaning toward reflection, subtlety and inward growth. Yin encourages you to step back, to embrace the quiet, to find strength in stillness. Combined with the intuitive wisdom of the Snake, this year offers an opportunity to listen deeply to the whispers of your inner world and move forward with purpose and clarity.

The Five Elements: Cycles of Growth and Renewal

The Five Elements—Wood, Fire, Earth, Metal, Water—are dynamic forces, each influencing and nurturing the next in an endless cycle.

Wood symbolizes growth, creativity, and expansion. It is the energy of spring, when life bursts forth with vibrant potential.

Fire represents passion, action and intensity, roaring to life in the heat of summer.

Earth grounds us in late summer, offering stability, nourishment, reflection. A time to harvest what we've sown.

Metal brings clarity and refinement in autumn, cutting away the unnecessary, focusing on what matters most.

Water flows through the depths of winter, embodying intuition, introspection, quiet renewal.

The Year of the Wood Snake, infused with the creative energy of Wood and the reflective nature of Yin, urges you to embrace growth that is deliberate and meaningful. A year to plant the seeds of what you want to create in your life and nurture them with patience and care.

The Chinese Zodiac: Animals as Archetypes

The twelve animals of the Chinese zodiac; Rat, Ox, Tiger, Rabbit, Dragon, Snake, Horse, Goat, Monkey, Rooster, Dog, and Pig, are more than just symbols. They are archetypes embodying unique traits, challenges and gifts. These celestial companions offer a lens through which to view the energies of each year.

The Snake slithers in on 29th January 2025 and will be fully emerged by 4th February. Snake is mysterious, intuitive and strategic. It doesn't rush, it waits, observing its surroundings- moving only when the moment is right. Paired with the vitality of Wood, the Snake's energy this year is one of transformation through deliberate action. It's about shedding old skins, embracing renewal and stepping into your future with clarity and purpose.

Seasons and Energies: Living the Dao through the Year

In Daoist thought, the energies of the year are reflected in the natural cycles of the seasons. Each season's element has particular energetic characteristics to guide you:

Winter: Water

A time of rest, introspection, reflection, restoration, renewal. This is a time to pause to listen to your inner self and dream of what's to come.

Spring: Wood

The season of growth, creativity, new beginnings. A time to plant seeds, both literally and metaphorically. A time for planning and taking the first steps toward your goals.

Summer: Fire

A phase of passion and action. Energy peaks and creativity flourishes. It's the moment to express yourself boldly and pursue your dreams wholeheartedly.

Late Summer: Earth

A transitional period of stability and grounding. It's the season to harvest the fruits of your endeavours and reflect on your progress. A time to find balance while you assimilate your new understanding into your life.

Autumn: Metal

A time of refinement and clarity. As the leaves fall from the trees, autumn invites you to let go of what no longer serves you and focus on what truly matters.

The seasons can appear mere markers of time however they are each a unique invitation to align with the natural flow of energy around you. Lean into the energies of each phase to support your personal and creative growth.

The Year of the Wood Snake: A Cosmic Blueprint for Transformation

The Year of the Wood Snake is a beautiful convergence of energies. A Yin year infused with the Snake's wisdom and the creative vitality of Wood. A year for peeling back the layers of the old and planting the seeds of the new. The Snake reminds you that transformation is a process, not a single moment. It's about moving with purpose, letting go of what no longer fits, leaving behind that which you have outgrown and embracing the mystery of what lies ahead.

As you step into this year of growth and renewal, take a moment to pause. Feel the rhythm of the natural world, tune in to the season and the quiet wisdom of the Snake coupled with the creative promise of Wood. With each of the coming seasons, the energy of the five elements and every journal entry allow yourself uncover and discover truths within yourself.

The dance has already begun. It's your turn to join in.

Chapter 1
The Year of the Wood Snake: A Year of Transformation and Growth

The Year of the Wood Snake beckons you in. With the allure of a secret garden at twilight, the air humming with the quiet promise of transformation. Not shouting nor demanding attention, instead this year begins unfolding softly. A Yin year led by the intuitive and enigmatic Snake, intertwined with the creative and expansive vitality of Wood. Together, they create a landscape ripe for personal growth, spiritual depth and deliberate meaningful change.

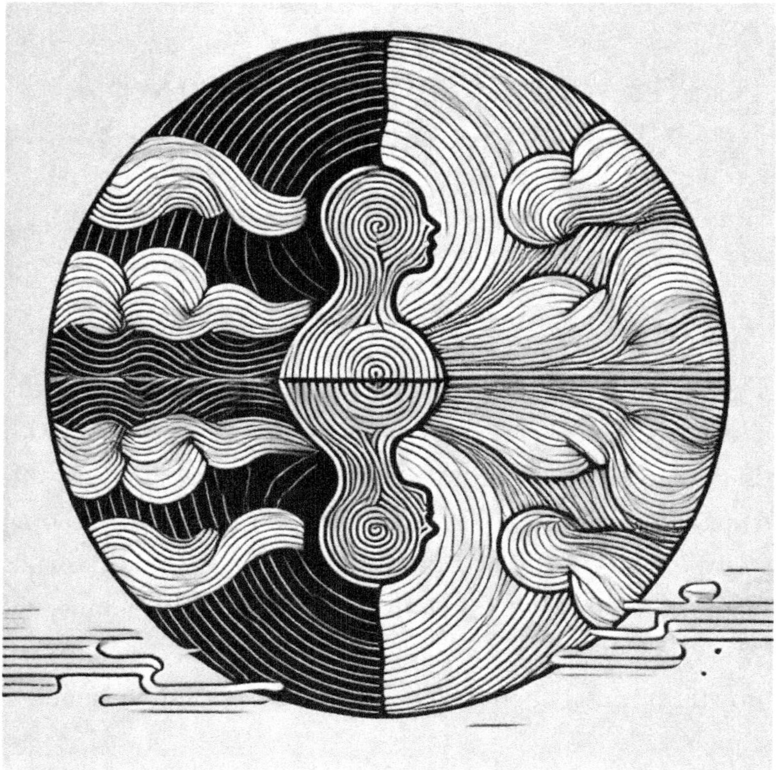

The Yin Essence: Strength in Stillness

Yin energy can feel mysterious, quiet and deep. It is the receptive half of the Yin-Yang balance, embodying qualities of introspection, intuition and subtle strength. In a world that often glorifies constant action and relentless productivity Yin quietly asks us to slow down, breathe and turn inward.

The Year of the Wood Snake amplifies this Yin quality. It's a time to cultivate stillness and reflect on the layers of your life that have perhaps gone unnoticed. Instead of rushing forward, this year invites you to pause and consider the terrain beneath your feet. What paths have brought you here? What burdens are you ready to set down? Yin reminds you that rest is not idleness it is preparation for the journey ahead.

Transformation comes through grace not force. The snake coiled and waiting demonstrates there is power in restraint, in knowing when to observe and when to act. 2025 is a year to trust slower and quieter processes. Utilizing methods that seem to happen beneath the surface, a place where roots grow unseen.

The Energy of Wood: Expansive Growth

Comparatively Yin energy is the stillness of the forest while Wood energy is the tree growing skyward. Wood energy is dynamic, brimming with vitality and creativity. It is the energy of growth, sometimes wild, if left unchecked or in deliberate and purposeful strides when wisely used. Wood nurtures innovation, resilience and the courage to start anew.

In the Year of the Wood Snake, the energy of Wood brings a sense of renewal to the Snake's introspective nature. Wood energy transforms reflection into action, urging you to plant seeds in the form of ideas, intentions and dreams. Allow these opportunity to take root and they will flourish over time. In the Yin Snake year Wood's growth is not hurried. Just as a tree grows year by year wood energy of the Yin Snake year can have a slow and steady expansion. The energy of Wood also encourages flexibility; the tree that bends with the wind. In 2025 you will be called to move with adaptability, so be ready to get flexible. Life may throw unexpected twists your way, however the Wood Snake's wisdom lies in knowing when to pivot, when to hold firm and when to let go. It's a dance of resilience and creativity, a reminder that growth doesn't have to be linear to be progressive and meaningful.

The Snake: A Guide to Transformation and Mystery

The Snake is one of the most fascinating and misunderstood archetypes of the Chinese zodiac. It is a creature of wisdom, strategy and mystery. Unlike the boldness of the Dragon or the exuberance of the Monkey, the Snake moves quietly, observing, waiting and conserving its energy for the perfect moment.

The Snake's energy in this year encourages transformation. This won't be an overnight process in the year of the Snake. Just as a snake sheds its skin, personal transformation in 2025 will not be a hasty process. Rather it will be deliberate, purposeful and above all necessary. The old is cast off to make way for the new. Leaving behind what has been outgrown. This symbolic act of renewal defines the essence of the Wood Snake year.

This energy in 2025 is about peeling back the layers of your life to reveal what is truly your authentic self. This is a time for asking big questions: What no longer fits? What truths are you ready to claim? The Snake invites you to embrace change, not as something to fear but as an essential part of your growth and evolution.

Yin + Wood + Snake: A fine combination

When Yin, Wood, and the Snake come together, they create a beautiful transformative potential. Yin's introspection, paired with Wood's creativity, makes 2025 a time for deep, meaningful exploration. The Snake adds its wisdom and mystery, urging you to approach life with strategy and purpose.

This unique combination means that the energies of the year won't be loud or overwhelming but steady and profound. It's not a time for impulsive action or rash decisions. Instead, it's a year to embrace thoughtful growth, to move with intention, and to trust in the process of transformation.

When a seed planted in fertile soil at first it appears that nothing is happening. However beneath the surface, roots are growing, finding nourishment and strength. Eventually, the seed breaks through the surface, and what emerges is new full of life and possibility. That is the energy of the Wood Snake year—a quiet yet powerful unfolding.

Practical Wisdom for the Year of the Wood Snake

To harness the energies of 2025 begin by aligning yourself with the natural rhythms of the seasons.

- **Slow Down and Reflect:** Give yourself permission to rest, to pause, and to take stock of where you are.

- **Suggested practices:** Journaling, silent meditation, walks in nature

These gentle activities help you to connect with the Yin essence of the year.

- **Plant Seeds of Intention:** What do you want to grow in your life?

- **Suggested practices:** Journaling, Free flow writing, daydreaming

These activities will help you gain clarity on what you want to grow in your life. Whether it's a creative project, a new skill, or a personal goal, this is the year to lay the groundwork in readiness for the fast pace year of the Fire Horse in 2026.

- **Embrace Transformation:** Like the Snake shedding its skin, let go of what no longer serves you. This could mean releasing old habits, relationships, or beliefs that hold you back.

- **Suggested practices:** Journaling, life story writing, editing previous writing, ritual and ceremony

These activities help you to embrace change and honestly examine what you have outgrown.

- **Stay Flexible:** Life can shift unexpectedly, lean into wood energy for flexibility and adaptability. Trust that growth often comes in ways you didn't anticipate.
- **Suggested practices:** Journaling, crosswords and puzzles, body movement such as Qi Gong, Yoga, Tai Chi and dance, swimming

These activities help you to remain flexible in mind and body.

- **Move with Intention:** The Snake's wisdom lies in knowing when to act and when to wait. Be deliberate in your choices, and trust your intuition to guide you.
- **Suggested practices:** Journaling, guided walking meditation, transformational or intuitive painting, body movement such as Tai Chi walking

These activities help you to gain a deeper awareness of moving with intention.

A Year to Grow, Reflect and Transform

The Year of the Yin Wood Snake brings with it a clear invitation. It is an opportunity to step into a year of quiet yet profound personal transformation and growth. Yin calls us into introspection and patience. The Wood energy inspires creativity and growth. While the Snake offers wisdom and the courage to embrace change. Together they create a blueprint for a year of deliberate, meaningful progress. This is not a year to rush or force outcomes. It is a time to honour the slow, steady unfolding of life's processes. To trust that even the smallest steps can lead to great transformations. As you move through 2025, let the energies of the Yin Wood Snake guide you toward growth, renewal and a deeper more profound connection with yourself and the world around you.

Chapter 2
Your Journal as a Compass for Self-Discovery and Creativity

Your journal is more than a collection of pages, it is a compass, a trusted guide through the twisting paths and open landscapes of the Year of the Wood Snake. A space where your thoughts can breathe, your dreams can take shape and your creative spirit can roam free. A journal isn't just a record of where you've been it's a map of where you're going and a mirror reflecting who you are in those moments

In 2025, with its Yin energy and the Snake's transformative wisdom, journaling becomes a profound act of self-discovery. It's a way to slow down and listen, to sift through the noise of the outside world and uncover the quiet truths within. At the same time, it's a spark for creativity, a place where ideas can germinate and grow, nourished by the expansive energy of Wood. This chapter will show you how to use this journal not just as a tool but as a companion for this unique year.

Journaling as a Ritual: Creating Sacred Space

Journaling is a ritual. Ritual doesn't have to mean candles and incense although it can be that. Treating your journaling as a sacred ritual is about making your writing practice intentional. Set aside a time that is non-negotiable, as little as 7 minutes a day can be beneficial. You may prefer the early morning as the world wakes, or late in the day when stillness wraps itself around you. Choose a space that feels inviting, whether it's a cosy nook by the radiator or a spot by a window full of light, have a place that is your writing place.

The act of journaling is both simple and deeply profound. Choose a journal that calls to you, you'll be more likely to stay consistent in your practice if you like your chosen journal and use a pen that you enjoy writing with. To activate your sense of flow try to use a journal that is landscape in orientation. This means there are less interruptions in your writing flow as you move further across the page before needing to move down. Using a blank page journal rather than one which is lined gives a further sense of freedom.

Experiment with your journaling ritual until your find your particular preferences. If you're wondering where or how to start begin by experimenting with this sequence:

- Open your journal.
- Take a slow breath in through your nose, hold that breathe for a moment before gently breathing out through your nose.

- Feel the weight of the pen in your hand, the texture of the page beneath your fingertips.
- Begin writing without any specific goal of writing something perfect or profound. Simply write with the intention of showing up for yourself.
- This is your space, your time.

It may be helpful to set a timer, this can help you to relax into and fully focus on your writing without worrying that you'll miss the bus or forget to pick up the children from school. How long you journal for is up to you. Experiment with different lengths of time to see what suits you best. Remember this may change over the year and as little as seven minutes journaling per day is beneficial.

Writing for Self-Discovery: Questions and Curiosities

The Year of the Wood Snake is one of reflection and growth. Use your journal to dive deep into the layers of your inner world.

Ask Questions, Don't Demand Answers

What am I feeling right now?

What do I truly desire?

What am I afraid to admit to myself?

Asking open-ended questions invites honesty and curiosity. Your journal isn't here to judge or solve but to listen. Sometimes the act of writing the question is more revealing than finding the answer.

Track Your Transformations

The Snake offers a reminder that shedding the old is part of growth. Journaling can help you to notice what you're outgrown and what you have left or are ready to leave behind. Notice, without criticising yourself, what patterns are reoccurring in your journal. Are you repeatedly referring to habits, relationships, beliefs that your journal is showing you is the skin to be shed? Your journal can also indicate what you are ready to embrace and the quiet calling of your future self which is beckoning your forward. Your journal is a place to be real, raw and honest. Write about any fears you may experience as part of your growth process and write in celebration of the joy and exhilaration that can come with change. Transformation isn't always clean or linear, your journal is a safe place to explore the messiness and the reality of it all.

JOURNAL

Find Patterns in the Chaos

Over time, your journal entries may reveal patterns; recurring thoughts, emotions, hopes, ideas and dreams. Pay attention to these threads as they are oftentimes pointing to something deeper that is asking for your attention.

Writing for Creativity: A Playground for Ideas

The Wood energy of 2025 is all about growth and creation. Your journal can be the soil where your ideas take root. Let it be messy, experimental, and free.

Free Writing: Release the Inner Critic

Start with a blank page and write whatever comes to mind. Don't worry about grammar, spelling, or coherence. Let your pen move as fast as your thoughts. This exercise clears mental clutter and often uncovers unexpected gems.

Mind Mapping: Connecting the Dots

Use your journal for mind maps; visual webs of ideas that help you see connections. Start with a central idea such as "What inspires me?" or "New project ideas" then allow your thoughts to flow and branch out from there. This is where creative sparks can fly. Remember it doesn't have to look neat and it doesn't need to appear logical.

Sketches and Doodles: Moving Beyond Words

Our first language as humans is one of imagery, returning to this pattern of representations can provide insights without the words getting in the way. Use your journal to sketch, doodle, or create abstract shapes. Visual expression taps into a different part of your creativity, one that requires less structure and is more instinctual.

Dream Journaling: Mining the Subconscious

The Snake thrives in mystery and so do your dreams. Keep your journal by your bed and jot down any dreams or fragments that linger upon waking. They might not make immediate sense, however over time patterns and symbols emerge. The very act of putting a dream journal by your bed and setting the intention to record your dreams seems to magically help in the recall and remembering of dreams. Your dreams can offer inspiration and insight, they are worth investigating.

Creative Challenges: Set Goals, Break Rules

Dedicate a page of your journal each week to a creative challenge. Write a poem, sketch a scene or brainstream an idea in seven minutes. The goal is to play and to explore not to create something perfect. Challenge yourself to unleash your creativity, break rules and PLAY.

Reflection: Looking Back to Move Forward

Journaling can be used to off load how you feel in the moment, to dream and plan your future and to reflect on the past. Reflection can be in the form of looking back on your life, telling your life story in the pages of your journal. Be aware of any tendency to beat up any previous version of you. Your reflective journal pages are not intended to be a stick with which to beat yourself. Taking an honest and objective look at your past without blaming yourself or others can help you gain a new perspective on old wounds. Reflection may also mean looking back through previous journal entries to discover patterns or recurring themes. This can help in discovering a deeper meaning and symbolism in your writing. Set aside time each month to read over your entries, ideally allowing the passage of three months between writing and reading. Highlight phrases or ideas that stand out. What surprised you? What patterns do you notice? What themes are emerging? Reflection helps you see how far you've come and offers clarity for where you may wish to go.

Journaling as Connection: Bridging Inner and Outer Worlds

In a year so deeply rooted in introspection and creativity journaling can be a bridge. It connects your inner world of thoughts, emotions, and dreams with your outer world of action and expression. As you write in your journal you are not simply recording aspects of your life, you are shaping your life. Discovering who you are, what you love, what you're capable of becoming and crafting your path forward.

Journaling meets you where you are. You can come to your journal as you are, starting from right where you are. At times your journal will be a place to vent frustrations, unravel worries and describe your current challenges. On other occasions it will be home to your brilliance and magnificence with abundant inspiration and that idea you never saw coming. No matter where you are in the moment your journal is there, your trusted companion, ready to receive and hold your words and sketches.

The Year of the Wood Snake: A Journey Unfolding

The Year of the Wood Snake offers energies that blend introspection, creativity, and transformation. This journal is your confidante for the journey. A place to explore, question, dream, and create. Allow yourself the freedom to let go of any need to fill the pages with perfect words, profound ideas and instantly publishable writing that really isn't how journaling works. Let your journal pages be an honest reflection the beautiful complexity of all aspects of your life.

Open your journal and let the adventure begin. Write freely, dream boldly, and discover the layers of yourself that are waiting to be uncovered and rediscovered. The Snake moves with purpose, the Wood grows with patience and you, with pen in hand, are ready to weave the story of your year.

Chapter 3
The Wood Snake: A Year of Growth, Mystery, and Transformation

To journey with the Wood Snake is to step into a world of quiet power and profound depth. The Snake is not loud nor brash. Its essence is like the whisper of wind through the forest, often unseen and yet present. The archetype of Snake holds mystery and wisdom. It is a guide through transformation that is unhurried, unfolding with deliberate purpose. The year of the Wood Snake gifts us a year rich in introspection, creativity and the slow, steady unravelling of life's deeper truths.

The Snake: Keeper of Wisdom and Transformation

The Snake is perhaps the most enigmatic of the Chinese zodiac animals. It slithers through life with a quiet confidence, observing and waiting before striking with precision. Snakes do not waste energy on the unnecessary, their movements are calculated, purposeful and deeply intuitive.

The Snake is associated with wisdom, strategy and transformation. Unlike the bold Dragon or the playful Monkey, the Snake operates in the shadows, valuing subtlety over spectacle. It is a creature of mystery, often misunderstood but endlessly fascinating to those willing to look deeper.

Transformation is central to the energy of the Snake. Shedding its skin is a physical and symbolic act of renewal. The Snake teaches us that growth often requires letting go, shedding the old to make space for the new. This is not a rushed process. The Snake knows the value of timing, of patience, of waiting for the right moment to move.

The Snake also carries an aura of magnetism. Its charm is not overt but compelling, drawing people in with its quiet allure. There's a depth to the Snake's energy that invites introspection, a pull to explore the unseen layers of life and self.

The Energy of Wood: Growth, Vitality, and Creativity

Wood is the energy of growth, things bursting into life, dynamic, expansive and full of vitality. The seed pushing through the soil, the sapling stretching skyward. Where the Snake might normally coil and wait Wood energy urges it forward, encouraging exploration and creativity.

Wood brings vitality to the Snake's wisdom. It fuels innovation and adaptability, making 2025 a year for creative breakthroughs and new beginnings. This energy is not about reckless expansion however. Wood is rooted in stability, growing steadily and purposefully. It reminds us that true progress comes from a strong rooted foundation.

The collaboration between the Snake and Wood creates a wonderful blend of introspection and outward growth. This is a year to reflect deeply on where you've been and use that wisdom to chart your new course. The Snake's strategic energy pairs perfectly with Wood's creativity, making this an ideal time to envision and lay the groundwork for long-term goals.

Yin Energy: The Quiet Force

As if the combination of Wood and Snake wasn't potent enough, the year's Yin quality adds another layer of depth. Yin energy is soft, receptive, and introspective. In a world that often glorifies action and noise, Yin reminds us of the power of stillness. The essence of the quiet strength of the moon silently pulling the tides or the calm within the storm.

The Yin aspect of the Wood Snake year encourages a different kind of growth—one that is less about external achievement and more about inner transformation. It's a year to listen more than you speak, to observe before you act, and to trust the subtle rhythms of your intuition.

Yin energy also heightens the Snake's natural tendencies toward reflection and strategy. It's a time to embrace patience, to sit with questions rather than rush to answers. The wisdom of the Snake, combined with the quiet force of Yin, invites you to delve into the deeper layers of your life, uncovering truths that may have been hidden or overlooked.

The Energetics of the Wood Snake Year

The energies of the Snake, Wood and Yin create a year unlike any other. An alchemical blend of transformation, creativity, and introspection. The Wood Snake Year occurs only once every 60 years, the last in 1965 and the next in 2085.

How will these coexisting energies will shape the year?

Intuition and Insight:

The Snake's natural intuition is heightened by Yin energy, making 2025 a year for deep insights. Trust your gut instincts. Don't be afraid to explore the unknown.

Purposeful Growth:

The Wood element fuels progress and the Snake's strategic nature ensures this growth is deliberate. This is not a year for rash decisions but for thoughtful planning and steady action.

Transformation through Shedding:

Just like a Snake shedding its skin, this year is about releasing what no longer serves you. It's a time to let go of old unhelpful habits, relationships that you no longer receive mutual nourishment from, or beliefs you have outgrown. Now is the time to let go of those layers to allow yourself to step into a new version and sense of who you truly are.

Creative Potential:

The vitality of Wood paired with the Snake's wisdom makes this an extraordinary year for creativity. Whether it's artistic expression, problem-solving, or innovation 2025 offers fertile ground for seeding ideas and bringing plans into being in a deliberate unrushed way.

Patience and Precision:

Yin energy tempers Wood's dynamism, reminding you to move with care. The Snake thrives on timing and precision. This year encourages you to embrace the art of waiting for the right moment.

Influences of the Wood Snake in Daily Life

THE ENERGIES OF THE WOOD SNAKE RIPPLE THROUGH all aspects of life. In relationships 2025 will encourage deeper connections, fostering intimacy and understanding. The Snake's charm and Wood's energy enabling collaboration make it an ideal time to strengthen bonds and build meaningful partnerships.

In work and personal projects leaning into to the strategic energy that 2025 offers is vital. This is a time for long-term planning, for laying the groundwork for future success that will unfold over years rather than weeks. Although creativity within these projects will flourishes, due to Wood energy influence, discipline and focus will be required to bring visions to life.

On a personal level the Wood Snake invites introspection. It's a year to ask big questions about who you are and where you're going. The answers may not come all at once, but the process of exploring them will bring clarity and purpose.

The Gift of the Wood Snake Year

The gift of the Wood Snake year is in an energetic environment that encourages you to slow down, reflect and grow in ways that are deliberate and meaningful. 2025 is a year for shedding old skins, releasing that which you have outgrown, planting new seeds and trusting in the powerful process of quiet transformation. The Snake doesn't rush and neither should you. This year isn't about quick fixes or flashy accomplishments. It's about the slow, steady unfolding of something deeper; a journey into yourself, guided by the wisdom of the Snake, the vitality of Wood, and the quiet strength of Yin. As you move through 2025 allow the energy of the Wood Snake to guide you. Embrace its wisdom, trust in its timing and allow the prevailing energies to shape your year into one of profound transformation and growth. This is your year to evolve, with grace not haste.

This is your year to evolve;
with grace not haste.

Chapter 4
The Snake in the Chinese Zodiac: Keeper of Mystery, Wisdom, and Transformation

The Snake slithers through the Chinese zodiac with a grace that's almost hypnotic. It doesn't rush, it doesn't stumble, moving with an otherworldly elegance, each movement calculated and deliberate. To understand the Snake is to venture into a world of nuance and depth, a world where intuition and strategy reign, where transformation is not just possible it is inevitable. The Snake is not loud or flashy, however its presence is impossible to ignore. It draws you in quietly, persistently, with the promise of truths just out of reach.

The Snake is the sixth sign in the Chinese zodiac, nestled between the boldness of the Dragon and the vitality of the Horse. Yet, it is entirely its own creature, embodying traits that are both beguiling and enigmatic. To know the Snake is to delve into its complexity, to understand its strengths, its shadows and the wisdom it offers to those who are willing to look beyond the surface.

A Creature of Intuition

At its core the Snake is deeply intuitive. It doesn't rely on brute force or sheer energy to navigate the world. It listens; to the whispers of the wind, to the subtleties of human interaction, to the unspoken truths which others may miss. The Snake's intuition is a sixth sense that allows it to read between the lines and anticipate what's to come.

This intuitive prowess makes the Snake a natural strategist. It doesn't act impulsively, instead observing and planning; waiting for the precise moment to strike. In any aspect of life; relationships, careers, creative endeavours and more the Snake's ability to see the bigger picture and move with purpose is supreme.

The Wisdom of the Snake

Wisdom is the Snake's defining characteristic. This is not the kind of wisdom that comes from textbooks or lectures. This is an inner wisdom culminated through experience, patience and looking inward. The Snake understands the value of self-reflection and the power of silence. It knows that profound and powerful insights can come through stillness rather than action.

This wisdom gives the Snake a magnetic quality. People are drawn to its depth, its ability to see the world from angles that could easily be overlooked. The Snake often plays the role of a confidant, a keeper of secrets, someone who can offer clarity in times of confusion. However although the Snake is generous with its insights, it is also fiercely protective of its own inner world. Trust must be earned, although even then the Snake rarely reveals everything.

The Transformational Power of Shedding

The visual image of a snake shedding its skin is a profound metaphor for transformation. The Snake understands that growth requires letting go. In order to step into something new you must first release what no longer serves you, that which you have outgrown. This process may not always be a comfortable one, however the Snake embraces it with quiet courage. The transformative energy of the Snake is a reminder that change is necessary and beautiful. This is an essential evolution towards becoming your true authentic self. Every ending is also a beginning the act of shedding, though it may sometimes be painful, anxiety provoking or uncomfortable, is ultimately what allows you to grow.

The Dual Nature of the Snake

The Snake has its shadows. Its depth and intuition, while powerful, can sometimes lead to overthinking or mistrust. The Snake's ability to see hidden truths can make it suspicious, frequently questioning the motives of others. This wariness, although useful and protective at times, can in some circumstances create barriers to connection. With a proclivity for strategy the Snake can veer into manipulation if unbridled. Snake energy has an ability to charm and influence therefore it is important to be mindful of this quality. The gifts and qualities of Snake must be considered with integrity using the insights to uplift rather than control. Despite these challenges the Snake offers many lessons. Teachings of the Snake include the importance of balance, remaining grounded and embracing both your light and shadow. 2025 is an excellent year to consider these lessons within your own life. It is the complexity of the Snake energy that makes it so compelling; a gentle reminder there is strength and growth to be found in acknowledging and integrating every part of yourselves.

The Charm of the Snake

The Snake has an undeniable allure, a magnetic quality that draws people in. This charm is not loud nor ostentatious. It is beautifully subtle, the Snake's charm is that whisper in a crowded room that makes you lean in closer. This is a magnetic quality born of authenticity, depth combined with an ability to make others feel seen and understood. The Snake is a natural storyteller, weaving words and ideas into something captivating. Its creative energy, fuelled by Wood in 2025, together with the ability to bring visions to life in a measured strategic way is an energetic that can support your forward movement and growth quietly and consistently throughout the year. The Snake certainly knows how to leave an impression so whatever your chosen medium; art, writing, conversation, leadership, career tap into this energy throughout 2025 to create an inspiring influence for those around you.

Relationships and the Snake

In relationships, Snake energy is deeply passionate and loyal, while also valuing its independence. It doesn't rush into connections, choosing its companions carefully. Once trust is established, the Snake is a devoted partner, offering depth, intimacy, and understanding. However the intensity of Snake energy can sometimes be overwhelming. Craving depth can create a struggle with superficiality. There can be an expectation of equivalent levels of commitment and authenticity from others. The Snake's journey in relationships is one of balance; learning to trust, to let go of control, and to embrace vulnerability.

Role of the Snake within the Chinese Zodiac

The Snake serves as a guide; a reminder to slow down, to look inward, to trust the process of transformation. It balances the exuberance of the Dragon and Monkey with its quiet depth, offering a counterpoint to the more action-oriented energies of the zodiac. As the sixth animal in the cycle the Snake sits on the pivot point of the ever changing balance of Yin and Yang energies within any given cycle. The Snake's presence is a call to embrace life's mysteries. An invitation to shed what no longer serves, to trust your intuition, to move through the world with grace and purpose.

Embracing the Snake Within

Navigating this Snake year in 2025 invites you to embrace the lessons of this enigmatic creature. Listen to our inner voice, embrace transformation and trust your journey even when the path ahead may be unclear. The Snake is a master of balance, blending intuition with strategy, depth with charm, wisdom with transformation. The invitation in 2025 is for you to do the same. Honour the complexities of your own life while moving through the world with the quiet power and purpose of Snake energy. Embrace the mystery, wisdom, and capacity to shed and grow. Trust that this same transformative power; the ability to grow, evolve, to emerge stronger and wiser as your true authentic self is within you. Leaning into and embrace your inner Snake potential to attain consistent growth throughout 2025.

Chapter 5
The Wood Snake: Where Growth Meets Mystery

The essence of Wood energy is vital, expansive, bursting with creative potential. Imagine this Wood energy as it exists in nature- a forest in the spring as it is waking up, coming alive, packed with purpose and potential. Trees stretching skyward with unstoppable momentum their roots extending deep into the earth providing stability. When this force of Wood energy intertwines with the enigmatic energy of the Snake the result is a wonderful blend of growth, intuition, creativity and transformation. The energy of the Wood Snake is not content to stay where it is. This energy calls for action, however this is not frenetic. It is purposeful movement, growth with a plan, creativity with depth.

The Nature of Wood Energy: Growth, Vitality, and Vision

The Wood element is about growth, vitality and momentum. It is dynamic and alive, associated with the season of spring when life bursts forth after the stillness of winter. Wood energy is not only about exuberance, there are also aspects of resilience, adaptability and progress. Just as a tree bends to the wind, moving with the force rather than resisting it, flexibility is its strength. Wood is related to the direction of east, the sunrise and the energy of beginnings. Thriving on creativity and innovation Wood energy encourages bigger dreams, expansion of horizons and pushing past perceived limitations. With its connection to the eye and vision, Wood energy allows you to see possibilities and plan your path toward them. Wood is both a dreamer and a planner, embodying the perfect balance between imagination and execution.

Reflections on Wood Energy

Although associated with movement and creativity Wood can have a tendency to become stuck and may produce too many ideas to be manageable. If you are experiencing the 'stuckness' of stagnating Wood energy ask yourself

Do you need more rest or more movement / activity?

If you have more creative projects than it is possible to complete in a lifetime in is worth asking yourself?

If I never had the opportunity to
finish any of my creative projects,

Which project would I feel most upset
to leave incomplete?

How Wood energy Influences the Snake energy

The Snake's characteristics of intuition, strategy, transformation, patience and subtlety become more dynamic and expansive under the influence of Wood energy.

Amplifying Growth and Creativity

The Snake is a master of transformation; shedding its outgrown skin and moving forward renewed. Wood amplifies this trait, infusing the Snake with a drive for growth in all spheres; personal, creative, intellectual and beyond. In the Year of the Wood Snake growth is deliberate and meaningful, therefore cultivating a transformation that is lasting and profound. The Snake's intuitive wisdom pairs beautifully with Wood's innovative energy meaning 2025 can be a year for breakthroughs. This may manifest itself in beginning a new project, learning a new skill, or reimagining old patterns and ways of being. The year of the Wood Snake is inviting you to embrace your creative potential.

Adding Flexibility to Strategy

The Snake is known for its strategic mind, however it can become overly rigid at times. Wood energy brings with it an aspect of flexibility which encourages the Snake to adapt and pivot when necessary. Although the Wood Snake knows when to hold its ground and when to flow with change it is important to be mindful that Wood energy can also have a tendency to become inflexible and stuck. Be aware of any patterns of 'refusing to budge' during 2025.

Ask yourself :

Would I benefit from being more flexible in this situation?

REMEMBERING OF COURSE THAT THE ANSWER MAY BE no. Sometimes you just have to stand your ground.

Encouraging Vision and Long-Term Thinking

The Snake characteristic of being drawn to deep insights and hidden truths is enhanced by the forward-thinking perspective of Wood energy. The Wood Snake can focus on the here and now while also looking ahead and planning for the future. Leverage these energies in 2025 to allow yourself to see the bigger picture and lay the groundwork for long-term success.

The Energetics of the Wood Snake: How to leverage that energy in 2025

- **Purposeful Expansion:** Unlike some other growth-oriented combinations the Wood Snake doesn't expand recklessly. Guided by the Snake's wisdom and strategy growth is measured and intentional.

- **Creative Depth:** Wood brings an outward energy to the Snake's inward tendencies creating a balance between introspection and expression. 2025 is definitely a year to take your inner truths and transform these into something tangible.

- **Adaptability with Focus:** The Snake's patience and precision are complemented by Wood's adaptability creating a dynamic yet grounded energy. Just as the Snake moves with belly to the earth this is a time to move forward with confidence and flexibility while remaining grounded.

Teaching of the Wood Snake

The Year of the Wood Snake offers profound lessons for those willing to embrace its energy.

- **Growth Requires Roots:** Upward growth requires roots if that growth is to be sustainable. An aspect of the Snake's wisdom is in laying a strong foundation before moving forward. Be it in your personal life, career or creative pursuits, 2025 asks you to ensure that your roots are as strong as your ambitions.

- **Patience Fuels Progress:** The Snake moves with calculated deliberation while Wood thrives on steady growth. Together the Wood Snake emphasises that progress does not have to be fast to be meaningful. Trust the process this year and know that no matter how small, each step is bringing you closer to your dreams and goals.

- **Creativity is a Process:** Wood energy is inherently creative coupled with the Snake's introspection this adds a mysterious depth to the creative process. This year encourages you to approach your projects as a journey not a destination. Play with your creativity, experiment, explore allow your ideas to evolve organically and follow where they lead.

- **Transformation is a Practice:** Shedding an old skin, that which has been outgrown can feel daunting, however this is necessary for growth. Wood Snake energy brings a reminder that transformation is not a single event, it is an ongoing process and practice. Let go of things that no longer serve you, these may include beliefs, habits, situations and relationships. Trust that the space this release creates will be filled with something new that is more aligned with your future.

Embracing Wood Snake Energy

To align with the energy of the Wood Snake, focus on cultivating personal growth and tapping into your inner wisdom.

- **Set Intentions:** Take time to reflect on what you want to grow towards and into this year. Write down your intentions and revisit them regularly to ensure you keep your dreams and goals at the forefront of your mind. Making an 'action board' featuring visual representations of your dreams and goals can serve as both reminder and a motivator.

- **Be Adaptable:** Life can be unpredictable, lean into the adaptability and flexibility of Wood energy. Be open to changes in direction, moving with the precession of Snake energy while trusting that this combination of flexible adaptability and openness can lead to some surprising opportunities.

- **Engage Your Creativity:** Through art, writing, problem-solving or innovation be sure to make space for creative expression in 2025. Let the energy of Wood inspire you to try new things and explore uncharted territory. As you engage with this creative exploration allow the influence of Snake energy to help you shed any unhelpful beliefs related to your creative practice.

- **Trust the Process:** Growth will not always be visible during 2025, however that doesn't mean it isn't happening. Just as a tree grows silently, your progress may unfold in ways that may not be immediately obvious. Have faith in the unseen work taking place beneath the surface.

The Year of the Yin Wood Snake: Quiet Power and Purpose

The blending of the intuitive depth of the Snake with the dynamic energy of Wood is powerful. A year for shedding the old, planting new seeds and growing with purposeful intention. There is no need to be racing to the finish line, 2025 invites you to be consistently moving forward with grace, patience and purpose.

As you navigate your way through 2025, trust in the wisdom of the Snake, embrace the creativity of Wood and allow these energies to support and shape your year. Growth is a way of being, rather than a singular action, the Wood Snake invites you to step into a your personal growth with quiet power and power; to fully embody transformation and evolution on all levels.

Chapter 6
Yin Energy in the Year of the Wood Snake: Embracing the Quiet Force

Yin energy is soft, receptive and deeply intuitive. Yin is the world at twilight, as the sun dips behind the horizon and the air is heavy with stillness. The cool embrace of night after the heat of day and the quiet wisdom that arises when the world slows down. Yin is often the hidden half of existence, often overshadowed by the active more assertive Yang, however Yin is no less powerful. In 2025, this Yin energetic will be shaping how you approach life, creativity and self-discovery.

The Nature of Yin Energy

Yin is the receptive counterpart to Yang in the duality of Daoist philosophy. Where Yang is outward, forceful, action-oriented; Yin is inward, reflective, subtle. Yin is the fertile soil quietly and patiently nurturing the seeds of growth. Yin isn't demanding nor pushy; it cultivates, allowing things to unfold naturally in their own time. Yin is often associated with the moon, water and night-time; all symbols of calm introspection. Yin could be said to govern intuition, patience and emotional depth. In a world that often prioritises hustle and productivity, Yin reminds us of the value of stillness and pausing to listen to the quiet voice within. These qualities will be amplified in 2025 creating an environment where transformation happens through flow not force and through quiet intention rather than noise.

Yin Energy in the Year of the Wood Snake

The Yin nature of 2025 will profoundly shape the Wood Snake's influence. The introspective and wise nature of Snake energy will be deepened by the presence of Yin energy throughout the year. Utilise this energetic to slow down and connect with your inner world. 2025 is not a year to be pushing for immediate results. Instead it is a year to sit with questions and contemplations, to trust the process of transformation and to embrace the subtle yet powerful shifts happening beneath the surface.

Yin energy will soften the expansive energy of Wood, tempering growth with patience. Wood energy fuels creativity and innovation, leveraging the Yin energy of 2025 will ensure your growth is intentional and aligned with your deeper values. Thus creating a harmonious balance between action and reflection, creativity and contemplation.

Yin Energy and your Personal Practices

To align with the Yin energy of this year chose personal practices that are more introspective in nature. The Year of the Snake is a time for looking inward and exploring the depths of your emotions, thoughts and desires.

- **Embracing Introspection**

Yin energy encourages self-reflection. Journaling, meditation and other contemplative practices are powerful tools for discovering your inner truth and uncovering your authentic self in 2025.

Ask yourself:

Who am I becoming?

What do I truly want?

What do I need to release to grow?

Allow yourself time to simply sit with these questions without searching or grasping for answers. Yin energy allows space for uncertainty and nurtures the quiet unfolding of clarity over time.

- **Prioritizing Rest and Renewal**

AMONGST THE NOISE AND CONSTANT CHURN OF DAILY life, taking rest can be viewed as unproductive. However, rest is not a luxury it is an absolute necessity. Lean into the Yin nature of 2025 and make rest a priority. Rest can take many forms; sleep, relaxation, gentle body movement, meditation, reading or a creative practice that both relaxes and engages you. Be sure to allow yourself space to create moments of stillness in your day. Give yourself permission to recharge. The Snake moves with purpose; taking rest and pausing is not the absence of progress, it is a vital part of it.

- **Deepening Emotional Awareness**

Yin energy may heighten emotional sensitivity, meaning this year is ideal for exploring your inner emotional landscape. Pay attention to all of your feelings, both the pleasant and the uncomfortable ones. These feelings are messengers.

Ask yourself:

What is this feeling trying to show me?

If this feeling is a messenger, what message does it bring?

By leaning into this awareness, you can cultivate greater self-compassion and enhanced empathy for others.

Yin Energy and Creativity

Creativity flourishes in the nurturing stillness of Yin energy, differing from the potentially explosive bursts of Yang fuelled creativity. In 2025, creativity will be much more focused on depth rather than speed and more about process than outcome.

Enhance your creativity in 2025 by aligning with the Yin energy:

- **Tapping Into Intuition**

Yin creativity is deeply intuitive. Trust the quiet whispers of inspiration rather than forcing ideas into being. Let your creative process be guided by your deeper instincts. Don't be afraid to explore unconventional ideas or follow creative threads that may not have a clear destination.

- **Cultivating Patience**

In the fast-paced world of deadlines and deliverables there is a danger that creativity can feel hurried or rushed. Yin energy invites you to slow down, to give your ideas the time and space they need to grow. Allow your creative work to gently unfold at its own pace. Follow where it leads you.

- **Exploring Depth**

THE YEAR OF THE YIN WOOD SNAKE IS THE TIME TO GO deep. Rather than skimming the surface, dive deeply into the heart of your creative projects.

Ask yourself:

What is the essence of what I am trying to express?

What truths am I uncovering/ discovering through this creative work?

The cultivating nature of Yin energy will support you in your exploration, ultimately encouraging you to create with authenticity and vulnerability.

- **Nurturing Your Creative Self**

Yin energy is innately nurturing, meaning this is an ideal year to care for your creative self. Surround yourself with inspiration that lights you up; books, music, paintings, photographs, nature, whatever feeds your soul. Create space in your life where your creativity can flourish, free from judgment or pressure to perform.

The Gift of Yin Energy

The Yin energy in 2025 offers you an opportunity to step back from the noise of life and reconnect with what truly matters. This is a year to trust the quiet processes of your life, to find strength in stillness and wisdom in reflection. The outward appearance of growth and transformation isn't always one of action. Align with the Yin energy of 2025 and allow your inner evolution to outwardly appear as pausing, waiting listening and allowing. Many societies equate value with productivity, the Yin energy in the Year of the Snake offers you the reminder of an alternative; the ancient truth that by simply being, your very existence is enough. Embrace the Yin energy, allow it to guide you toward a deeper understanding of yourself, your creativity and the world around you.

Embracing Yin Energy in 2025

- **Create Space for Stillness:** Dedicate time each day to quiet reflection. This may be through meditation, journaling or sitting in silence

- **Honour Your Intuition:** Trust your inner voice, even when it challenges logic or convention.

- **Slow Down:** Resist the urge to rush. Allow yourself to move at a pace that feels natural and sustainable.

- **Nurture Yourself:** Treat yourself with care and compassion. Rest when you need to and allow yourself to say no to things that drain your energy.

- **Celebrate the Process:** Focus on the journey or process rather than the destination or outcome. This applies in both your personal growth and your creative endeavours.

A Year of Quiet Power

The Yin energy of 2025 is a quiet, persistent force silently shaping the world. That persistence is what allows water to carve a canyon. The quiet strength is the moon moving the tide. Yin holds a silent space for transformation. As you navigate the Year of the Wood Snake, embrace the softness, patience and wisdom of Yin energy. Trust that in the stillness, you will find everything you need through flow, not force. This is your year to grow, to create and to discover the profound power of that quiet force within you.

A Season of Growth and Possibility

The Wood Energy phase is a season of hope, creativity and boundless potential. A time to say your Sacred YES to growth, change and those dreams that make your eyes sparkle and your heart race. It is also a time for thoughtful cultivation. Your growth in the spring of 2025 is about nurturing not forcing. Trust that any small steps you take today will bloom into something bigger and bolder.

Allow yourself to be guided by curiosity and wonder. Let your creativity flow freely, unburdened by fear or doubt. Be adventurous and playful. Trust that within you lies that same vitality and deep knowing of purpose and direction as the trees and flowers bursting into life around you. This is your season to grow, create and to step into the light.

Chapter 7
Seasons, Energies and Spirit

The cycle of seasons within a year are what breathe life into the earth and move the energy of your soul. These five phases; winter, spring, summer, late summer, autumn move with their own unique energetic, essence and rhythm. They are so much more than simply markers of time. They influence nature and the human spirit, shaping not only the world outside but the landscapes of your inner life too. The Five Elements; Water, Wood, Fire, Earth, Metal are each associated with a unique energy and spirit. Always in constant dialogue, flowing into one another through a cycle of nurturing, at times regulating each other through the controlling sequence. This is an endless dance of creation and transformation. This is your invitation into the dynamism of the cycle, to feel its pulse and understand its influence.

Winter: The Energy of Water and the Spirit of Zhi (Willpower)

Winter arrives like a whisper, blanketing the world in stillness, this is the Water energy phase. The element of seeing the bigger picture, looking at resources and reserves, assessing safety on a personal level and beyond. The emotion of fear is associated with the Water element. The Spirit of Water energy is the Zhi (willpower). Zhi is not a forceful will, it is the unshakable resolve that arises from heartfelt purpose. It is the inner voice that gently urges "Rest now and do not give up". Winter is a time to turn your focus inward, allow yourself to reflect and recharge.

Ask yourself:

What is lying dormant within me, waiting to awaken?

What do I need to preserve and nurture in the depths of my Soul?

Spring: The Energy of Wood and the Spirit of Hun (Imagination)

In nature spring bursts forth in a riot of colour and life, a concerto of new beginnings. This is the Wood energy phase. The element of growth, vitality, dreaming and boundless imagination. The great potential in the energy of the Wood phase is demonstrated in nature, a seedling pushing its way up through the soil. Wood is dynamic, expansive and bursting with the promise of what could be. The emotion of anger is associated with the Wood element. The spirit of Wood energy is Hun (imagination), the ethereal soul that fuels your imaginings and your dreams. Hun is that creative force that paints vivid pictures in the mind and challenges with the question "What if?" Spring is a time to allow yourself to be inspired to reach beyond what is and envision what could be. Tap into the Wood energy of spring to set intentions and plant the seeds of your dreams.

Ask yourself:

What do I want to create?

What visions stir within me that are longing to take shape?

This is the season to embrace possibility, to dare to dream big and act boldly.

Summer: The Energy of Fire and the Spirit of Shen (Conscious Mind)

Summer comes blazing into being with warmth and vitality, lighting the world with passion and connections. This is the Fire energy phase. The element of love, illumination, joy and boundless energy. In nature fire illuminates; radiating both heat and light. Fire is the spark of life, the essence of movement and change. The emotion associated with Fire energy is joy. The spirit of Fire energy is the Shen (conscious mind). Shen is the light of awareness and aliveness, the sense of self that allows you to connect with others and the world around you. It's the part of you that laughs, loves and shines brightly when you are fully present. Summer invites you to live fully alive, to express yourself with joy and authenticity. Embrace the fire energy of summer to bring more joy into your life.

Ask yourself:

How can I share my light with the world?

What passions burning within me are demanding to be expressed?

This is a season for embracing life in all its vibrancy, for celebrating connection and possibility.

Late Summer: The Energy of Earth and the Spirit of Yi (Intellect)

Late summer is a moment of pause between summer and autumn a time of balance and fulfilment. This is the Earth energy phase. The element of nourishment, stability and harvest. In nature Earth energy is one of offering up the results of spring planting in abundance. Earth energy is grounding and supportive, an anchor that provides steady holding amid life's changes. The emotion associated with Earth energy is overthinking, which can be triggered by Earth energy's desire to understand and to be understood. The spirit of Earth energy is Yi (intellect and intention). Yi is the thoughtful, reflective part of you that analyses and makes sense of your world. It's that steady hum of thoughts weaving concepts into understanding and assimilating that understanding into your daily life. The phase of Late Summer is an invitation to pause and take stock.

Ask yourself:

What have I cultivated thus far in 2025?

What am I ready to harvest?

How can I bring balance and stability into my life?

How can I assimilate new understanding into my day to day life?

Autumn: The Energy of Metal and the Spirit of Po (Subconscious)

AUTUMN SWEEPS IN WITH A CRISP EDGE, THE SEASON OF refinement and release. This is the Metal energy phase. The element of clarity, seeing what's missing and what may be incomplete. In nature Metal energy is one of letting go; Trees push toxins into their leaves before allowing them to fall without resistance or trying to hold on. Metal is sharp and precise, cutting away the unnecessary to reveal what truly matters. The emotions associated with Metal energy are sadness and grief. The spirit of Metal energy is Po (the subconscious mind). Po is the primal, instinctive part of you, deeply connected to the physical body and the cycles of life and death. It is the voice that speaks from deep within, urging you to honour your instincts, let go and embrace transformation. The Autumn phase of the year is your invitation to release what no longer serves you.

Ask yourself:

What am I holding onto that I need to let go of?

How can I refine my focus and align with what truly matters to me?

This is a season for finding clarity in simplicity and strength in letting go.

The Five Energies in Harmony

Each of these seasonal phases with their associated energies are part of a larger cycle of life. Together they form a cycle of creation, growth, transformation, death and renewal:

Winter (Water/Zhi): Rest and reflection.

Spring (Wood/Hun): Growth and imagination.

Summer (Fire/Shen): Passion and connection.

Late Summer (Earth/Yi): Stability and understanding.

Autumn (Metal/Po): Clarity and release.

The five energies flow through the seasons as witnessed in the natural world. And these same energies are flowing through you. Individually and collectively the five energies can influence your thoughts, emotions and actions. This offers a framework for understanding and aligning with the rhythms of life.

JOURNAL

Living in Tune with the Seasons

Living in harmony with the five seasonal phases deepens your awareness of the shifting energies within and around you. Eating seasonal foods, dressing in line with the seasonal climate and self-cultivation practices that align with the energetic phase of the year can help you to attune and adapt to the changing energies within and around you.

Every season and its energy has a purpose within that season and as part of the larger cycle. The stillness of winter allows you to assess your reserves and resources, preparing you for spring's growth. The vitality of spring gives you momentum and inspiration that fuels summer's passion. The heat of summer brings joy and motivates connections, which then softens into late summer's grounding. Your assimilation of new understanding in late summer then surrenders to autumn's clarity. The releasing, letting go and simplifying in all aspects of your life in the autumn phase then leads you once again into the stillness and reflection of winter.

Allow the cycle of the seasons inspire and guide you. Rest in winter, dream in spring, shine in summer, assimilate in late summer, release in autumn. Trust that each phase has its purpose in your life. By moving with a seasonal flow, you can connect with your inner and outer worlds in a deeper more authentic way.

Chapter 8
The Water Energy Phase: Reflection and Intuition (December 2024 to February 2025)

The year begins with a whisper, the world feels quieter, the days still short and sharpened by winter's chill. This is the Water Energy phase: a time to slow down, turn inward and to listen to the subtle currents of your Soul. Water is the element of intuition, reflection and depth. Just as the river persists carving its path through stone, water energy has a quiet power that leaves its mark on everything it touches. During this phase your invitation is to pause, reflect and embrace the stillness. Using this still reflection as a mirror to observe your inner self. What truths lie beneath the surface awaiting discovery? What old fears, patterns or unhelpful habits are ready to be released? The Water Energy phase is a time for emotional rest and renewal, to check in with your personal reserves and resources. It is a sacred pause before the creative growth of the coming spring.

Reflection and Intuition: The Essence of Water Energy

Water energy is both still and flowing. Holding the paradox of stillness in movement and movement in stillness. Deeply restful and quietly transformative, inviting you to slow down and rest deeply, while also to remaining open to insights that come when busyness ceases and deep listening begins.

The Spirit of water energy is Zhi (willpower). This is a quiet determination of purpose, it is the sprig of plant life that pushes up through the pavement, knowing that it has a purpose- simply 'to grow'.

In this Water Energy phase allow reflection and intuition to be your central focus. Explore your inner world with curiosity and self-compassion, allowing yourself to gently and lovingly identify goals for emotional regulation, stability and well- being. Allowing the movement and flow of water to wash away that which no longer serves you. Lessons from your past become stepping stones for your future when viewed with self-compassion and loving kindness, rather than using past experiences as a stick with which to beat yourself in the present. Fears held by a previous version of you can be dissolved in the still waters of acceptance by the current version of who you are now and who you are yet to be.

Journal Prompts for Reflection and Intuition

Emotional Goals:

What are my emotional priorities for this year?

How can I cultivate a sense of peace and balance in my daily life?

What feelings do I want to experience more often in 2025? How can I create space for these feelings?

What loving boundaries do I need to set to protect my emotional well-being?

How can I deepen my relationship with myself through self-compassion?

Lessons from the Past:

What were the biggest emotional lessons I learned in 2024, the year of the Yang Wood-Dragon?

What moments from 2024 am I most grateful for? Why I am grateful for these moments?

How have my previous challenges shaped me into the person I am today?

What unhelpful patterns from my past do I notice I am repeating? How can I shift these unhelpful patterns into ones that support my growth and transformation?

Who or what supported me during challenging times in 2024? How can I express my gratitude?

Releasing Fears:

What fears or anxieties am I holding onto that I am now ready to let go of?

How have these fears served me in the past? In what way(s) are those fears no longer severing me now?

What small step can I take today to address one of my fears with courage and self-compassion?

What would my life look like if I no longer allowed unfounded fear to dictate my choices?

Who or what inspires me to be courageous? How can I draw on that inspiration in my daily life?

Intuition and Inner Wisdom:

What is my intuition telling me about the coming year?

When was the last time I trusted my 'gut instinct'? What resulted from that instinctive trust?

How can I create more space in my life to hear and honour my intuition?

What symbols, dreams and signs have appeared to me recently? If I knew what these were telling me, what would that message be?

What does my inner wisdom want me to know right now?

Looking Forward:

What aspects of me do I want to bring with me into the next phase of the year and what do I want to leave behind?

Based on my reflections and discoveries through journaling in this water phase what intentions do I now want to set for the coming wood phase of the year?

Using the Water Energy Phase for Emotional Rest and Creative Incubation

The Water Energy phase is an invitation to being without doing. A time to let go of the need for constant productivity and embrace the value of rest and reflection. Emotional rest is not a void without thought or feelings. While taking emotional rest it is important to hold a loving space for any thoughts and feelings that arise without judgment. Allowing any arising thoughts and feelings to flow like water onto the pages of your journal.

Creatively, the water phase is a fertile ground for incubation. Water feeds life, in this case starting to give life to your creative stirrings emerging from this time of stillness. Ideas may not yet be fully formed, hiding beneath the surface awaiting a more inviting climate. Use this time to mind wander, doodle and jot down fragments of thoughts without the pressure of turning them into something tangible yet. Like seeds lying dormant in winter, these creative sparks need time to gather strength before they break through the soil in spring.

Water energy is patient and persistent. It leaves its mark. A reminder that your growth and transformation does not have to be loud or fast to be meaningful. Trust in the stillness. Trust the process. Most importantly trust yourself. This is your time to rest and reflect allowing the quiet power of Water to guide you toward the next chapter of your unique journey.

Chapter 9
The Wood Energy Phase: Growth and Creativity (March to May 2025)

Spring arrives with a crescendo of new growth, a symphony of green unfurling in every direction. It is the season of possibility. The world shakes off the stillness of winter and bursts into life. Spring, the energetic phase of Wood is a time of growth, vitality and unleashing creative potential. The Wood Energy phase is generally not a time for hesitation. This energetic phase seeks movement and can spark your forward motion. Seeds previously planted, now gain the momentum to break through the soil and reach upward for the sun. Wood does not ask for permission to grow, it has a wonderful rebellious nature and holds an expansive energy. Therefore without being asked or given permission it grows, stretches, expands and transforms with relentless curiosity. Your invitation during this wood energy phase of spring aligns with this expansion and movement. Step into new beginnings, nurture the creative spark within and stretch beyond the boundaries of what you thought was possible.

The Nature of Wood Energy

Wood is dynamic. It thrives on movement, pushing upward and outward with a pulsating vitality. Wood energy can be chaotic and prone to getting stuck and stagnating. By becoming aware of any areas of chaos and stagnation within yourself and your life allows you to leverage the movement and expansion of wood energy to shift and transform. Thus your growth becomes more deliberate. Although the branches of a tree may appear to have grown in random directions, it has grown with purpose and direction, guided by the sun and anchored by its roots. Your invitation during this wood phase is to lean into the wood phase and leverage its vitality, creativity and expansive energy to curate your own unique path and transformational growth.

Wood holds the energy of imagination, exploration and expansion. Inviting you to imagine into your dreams, intentions and goals, expand your horizons and create with intention. This is a time to embrace possibility, innovate and to say yes to the things that spark your imagination and enliven your being.

Growth and Creativity in the Spring Phase

In this Year of the Yin Wood Snake the Wood energy of spring is complimented by the nurturing stillness of Yin and the strategic wisdom of the Snake. Your growth in this phase is not simply about expansion, this is a time for meaningful and deliberate progress. Focus your creativity on crafting something that resonates deeply with who you are. This is your invitation to step into the role of creator and cultivator.

Ask yourself:

What do I want to grow in my life?

What creative dreams stirring within me are waiting to be nurtured?

The time to imagine into and play with those dreams is now. Move forward with your dreams with purpose, not haste.

JOURNAL

Journal Prompts for Growth and Creativity

Setting Intentions:

What intentions do I really want to set for this season of growth?

How can I align my actions with my values to create meaningful progress?

What does "growth" mean to me right now? How can I embrace this meaning of growth in all aspect of my life?

What small steps can I take today to move closer to my dreams?

How can I make space in my life for the things that truly matter?

Nurturing Creativity

What creative project or idea have I been longing to start?

How can I create an environment that inspires and supports my creativity?

What does my inner artist need from me this spring?

What is holding me back from expressing myself creatively? Are these internal or external factors?

How can I bring more playfulness into my creative process?

Expanding Horizons:

What new experiences or challenges can I embrace to expand and change my perspective?

How can I gently push my growth edge, or move to the edge of my comfort zone this spring?

What skill or knowledge do I want to explore or develop?

Who inspires me? How can I learn from their journey?

What new connections can I make to broaden my personal or professional world?

Growth and Transformation:

What unhelpful patterns from the past am I ready to release? What helpful patterns do I want to embrace?

How have I already grown so far this year? What do I want to build on going forward?

What useful learning from winter can I carry forward into spring?

What do I need to let go of to make space for growth?

How am I choosing to celebrate the progress I've made?

Looking Ahead:

What long-term vision do I have for myself?

How can I take steps toward that vision during this season?

Leveraging the Vitality of Spring

THE WOOD ENERGY OF SPRING'S ENERGY IS MOST powerful when directed with intention. To harness this energy for personal and creative growth remember to;

- **Start Small, Dream Big:** Every tree begins as a seed. Break your big dreams into small manageable steps that feel achievable while keeping your larger vision in mind.

- **Create a Growth Environment:** Surround yourself with inspiration; books, music, people, art. Visit places that spark your curiosity and encourage your creativity.

- **Take Action: Growth requires movement.** Don't wait for the "perfect" moment to begin, you are ready now. Take your first step, you can adjust your direction as you go.

- **Celebrate Progress:** Acknowledge and celebrate all your achievements. Size does not matter. Every step is worth celebrating.

- **Stay Flexible:** Like the tree that bends without breaking in the wind be adaptable to changes and challenges as they arise. Growth is rarely linear so embrace any detours as opportunities to learn.

- **Make Time for Play:** Creativity thrives on playfulness. Give yourself permission to experiment, explore and make fabulous creative mistakes. It's all part of the process.

Stay Connected to Your Roots: While reaching for the sun and the stars it's important to remain grounded. Restate your personal values and ensure your growth aligns with what truly matters to you.

Chapter 10
The Fire Energy Phase: Passion and Connection (June to August 2025)

Summer arrives bold, exuberant and unapologetically alive. As daylight hours stretch, humming with possibility, the world leans into the anticipation of something amazing. This is the season of Fire energy filled with passion, playful action and connection. Fire ignites the spirit with a vitality that demands to be passionately felt, expressed and shared. This summer phase of the year is one to be played full out; not held back, muted or dampened. It's a time to live fully alive, embrace your heart's passions and allow yourself to shine. This exuberance is not to be mistaken for doing more to the point of exhaustion. This is the energy of doing what matters most to you and doing it with purposeful joy. The strategic wisdom of the Wood Snake guides you towards a summer of celebration that has within it a call to action and a heartfelt invitation to express who you are and what you stand for in the world. To make meaningful connections with like-minded Souls.

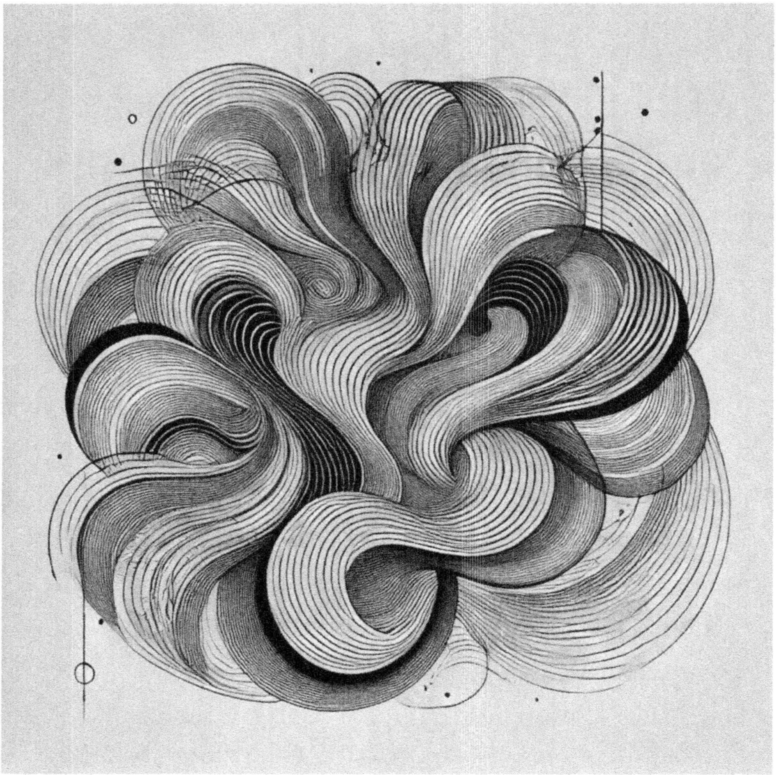

The Nature of Fire Energy

Fire is dynamic, transformative and can be hypnotic. It is the spark that ignites, the warmth that connects and the light that illuminates. Fire is the energy of passion, creativity and connection. The force that propels us to take risks of the heart, express ourselves boldly and to build meaningful connections. Fire energy requires a delicate balancing act. Too much will easily overwhelm, while too little will hide the joy and fun of life firmly out of sight. The challenge of this energetic phase of summer is to harness the power of Fire energy without allowing it to consume and burn you out. Instead, channelling its influence into pursuits that align with your deepest passions and values.

Shen is the Spirit of Fire energy. Representing the conscious mind, the Shen is the essence of presence and awareness. The light of understanding that enables you to connect deeply with yourself and others. Your invitation during summer is to engage fully with your life, to love fiercely and to express yourself with joy and authenticity. This is your permission slip to live boldly, investing time and energy into pursuing your passions and your desires. It is a time to shine a light into dark places, to speak your truth and to build connections that light your Soul with Fire's warm embrace.

This is a time to be showing up fully alive and taking guidance from your own inner flame of the heart. Let go of perfectionism and overthinking and follow your heart, it will light your way.

Fire Energy in 2025

In 2025 the exuberance of Fire energy is tempered by the wisdom of the Snake. This balance helps to ensure that your actions are intentional, guided by clarity and purpose rather than chaotic and reckless. Although passion is a potent fuel it is strategy and insight that will safeguard and sustain your inner flame.

Journal Prompts for Passion and Connection

Expressing Joy:

What brings me the most joy right now? How can I invite more of it into my life?

When was the last time I felt truly alive? What was I doing when I felt that aliveness?

How can I most usefully celebrate the small moments of happiness in my everyday life?

What does joy feel like in my body? How can I cultivate that sensation more often?

Who or what makes me smile and laugh? How can I express gratitude for their presence in my life?

Pursuing Passions:

What am I most passionate about? How can I dedicate more time to my passions this summer?

What is one dream I've been putting off? How can I take the first step toward that dream?

What creative project or idea excites me? How can I bring it to life?

How can I make space in my life for the things that truly light me up?

If success was guaranteed what passion of mine would I choose to pursue?

Choosing and Taking Risks:

What calculated risks am I willing to take to pursue my passions?

How can I move towards my growth edge in a way that feels both thrilling and safe?

What might happen if I take this leap? Why can I handle it?

What's the best that could happen if I dare to take a chance?

Who or what inspires me to live authentically? How can I draw on that inspiration in my daily life?

Connection and Expression:

What truths do I need to express? With whom do I need to share these truths?

How can I deepen my connection with the people who matter most to me?

What story or idea do I feel called to share with the world?

How can I use my voice and my creativity to make a positive impact in the world?

How can I more fully express my authentic self in my relationships, career and creative practice?

Looking Forward:

At the end of this summer what do I want to celebrate and feel proud of?

Embracing the High Energy of Summer

- **Follow Your Joy:** Let joy be your compass. Engage with activities, people and experiences that make you feel most alive.

- **Take Daring Action:** Fire energy is full of passion. Leverage this phase of the year to take action on your dreams. Trust the transformative nature of Fire as you move towards your growth edge.

- **Prioritise Connection:** Summer is a time for building and strengthening relationships. Enhance your bonds and connections with others by sharing your joy and passions. Express gratitude and loving kindness with integrity and honesty this summer.

- **Embrace Playfulness:** Allow yourself to play, experiment and enjoy the process of creativity with concern or focus on outcome. Make space for fun, letting go of seriousness and goal-orientation for a while.

- **Balance Passion with Rest:** Fire needs fuel or it will burn out. Ensure you make time to recharge and care for yourself so that your energy remains buoyant. Self-love and self-compassion are vital during this high energy phase

- **Be Present:** Fire energy loves to be fully engaged in the moment. Allow yourself to taste and savour the experiences of summer without rushing to get through as many as possible. Be conscious of your choices in selecting what you say yes to.

- **Let Your Light Shine:** Share your ideas, talents and authentic self with the world. You have something unique to offer, only you can show up as you in the world. Let yourself be seen.

The Fire Energy of summer is your invitation to live with passion and joy. To express yourself fully and embrace the vibrancy of life. This is the time to shine your light and to pursue what sets your heart ablaze. Leverage the expansive nature of Fire energy to connect authentically and deeply with the world around you. Take calculated risks by consciously selecting how much to say yes to. Explore your dreams through Fire's illumination, remembering to celebrate the beauty and joy of the moment. Paired with the wisdom of the Wood Snake your heart's passion can lead you exactly where you need to go.

Chapter 11
The Earth Energy Phase: Grounding and Stability (August to September 2025)

Late summer, the time of Earth energy, wraps the world in golden embrace, a season of quiet abundance and reassuring warmth. The frenetic energy of spring and summer softens, giving way to a time of assimilation and grounding. Late summer is an opportunity to pause, to harvest that which was sown in the wood energy phase of spring. Your invitation in late summer is to integrate new understanding and learning from the preceding seasons. Ask yourself how this new understanding can be assimilated into your daily life and your creative practice.

Earth Energy is an anchor in the cycle of the elements. The soil beneath your feet, a steady rhythm and place of safety. The calm arising from the knowledge you have done the work of previous seasons and can now begin to reap the results and rewards.

In this Year of the Wood Snake the Earth energy phase is a time to consolidate your growth and transformation of previous months, to understand how much you have grown and to find stability as you prepare for your next chapter.

Earth Energy is nurturing, grounding and stabilising. Representing a sense of centeredness, of being rooted even when life continues to shift around you. The essence of Earth energy is a place of fullness and abundance, rooted and steady. It is the tree heavy with fruit, deep roots holding firm in the soil as its branches bow with the rewards of thoughtful planting in spring and the loving energy of summer.

The Spirit of the Earth element

Yi, the intellect, is the Spirit of the Earth element. Yi facilitates processing and making sense of your experiences, allowing you to weave them into understanding and ultimately wisdom.

Ask yourself:

What have I learned?

What am I carrying forward?

What do I need to leave behind?

Late summer invites you to slow down and incorporate new understanding and learning into your daily life. This is a time of consolidation. Relax, take time to appreciate where you are and how you have grown over the year so far. Celebrate yourself and take pause amidst the whirlwind of life, enjoy some lazy days. The wisdom and strategy of the Snake align beautifully with the Earth energy phase, inviting you to solidify your learning and feel the support of the ground beneath you. This is your foundation for the coming season.

Journal Prompts for Grounding and Stability

Celebrating Growth and Achievements:

What am I most grateful to have accomplished so far this year? Why am I grateful for this?

How have I grown emotionally, spiritually and creatively since the start of 2025?

What challenges have I overcome and what strengths have I discovered in the process?

Who or what has supported my learning and understanding since the beginning of this Wood Snake year? How can I express gratitude?

What moments do I want to revisit and savour?

Cultivating Deeper Growth:

How can I bring more opportunities for growth and learning into my daily life through rest and pause?

What does "self-cultivation" mean to me? How can I practice this?

What small everyday moments bring me most harmony and restfulness?

How can I create space for physical, emotional, mental and spiritual nourishment in my routine?

What creative practices feel most nourishing to me?

Nurturing Community:

Who in my life deserves my attention and care right now?

How can I deepen my connections with the people I value most?

What relationships have nourished me this year? How can I show my appreciation?

What does a balanced and healthy relationship look like to me?

How can I be a source of grounding and support for others without over giving or sacrificing myself?

Assimilating and Understanding:

What have I learned from the challenges I've experienced this year?

How have my experiences shaped my perspective and priorities?

What habits, beliefs, situations and relationships no longer serve me now? How can I shed these?

What patterns or themes have emerged in my life? If I knew what these meant, what would their message be for me?

How can I integrate the insights I've gained and assimilate my new understanding into my daily life as I move forward? What actions do I need to take now?

Looking Ahead

Having taken my new understanding into account, how can I now prepare for the next phase of the year? Is there anything I still need to digest before moving forward?

Leverage Earth Energy's Grounding

- **Celebrate the Harvest:** Take time to acknowledge and celebrate your achievements. Assess the progress you have made and give yourself credit for the effort you've put in.

- **Reconnect with Your Roots:** Ground yourself by revisiting your values, intentions and the reasoning behind your actions. Use this phase to ensure that your growth remains aligned with what truly matters to you.

- **Create Space for Digesting and Processing:** Set aside quiet moments to process your journey thus far. Do this through a blend of journaling, meditation and walks in nature. Give yourself time to think, feel and integrate.

- **Nurture Your Relationships:** Leverage the stable grounding energy of Earth to deepen connections with the community around you. Strengthen your support system by reaching out and lean into the shared understanding of like-minded Souls.

- **Harvest what's useful, leave the rest:** Take what resonates and leave the rest. In preparation for the coming of autumn begin to clear space creating room for what is truly important to you. Let go of needing to understand everything all at once, the most needed answers will come in time.

- **Focus on Balance:** Your invitation in this phase of the year is to find your own equilibrium. Notice the balance you create between work and rest, giving and receiving, action and flow. Balance is not always symmetrical allow for more rest, receiving and organic flow when you need to. Life isn't always a 50/50 spilt, adjust in a way that restores your harmony.

- **Root Your Insights:** There is deep and valuable wisdom in your experiences of the past months. Use this phase of the Wood Snake year to consolidate your insights and learning. Root this wisdom into your everyday life to guide your onward journey and growth.

Late Summer

Late summer invites you to take pause amidst the rush of life, savour your achievements and ground yourself in the present moment. Time to process your new learning, connect and reconnect with your community and the values that matter most to you. Taking pause to process and assimilate will prepare your for the coming season of Metal energy.

Embrace the steady nourishment of Earth energy. Trust that in this quiet pause, you are gathering strength and wisdom to equip you for your future journey. Ground, consolidate and remember to celebrate yourself and your harvest.

Chapter 12
The Metal Energy Phase: Simplifying and Letting Go (October to December 2025)

Autumn arrives with crisp air carrying the scent of fallen leaves. Soft golden light of shorter days signals a shift into the phase of change, release and simplification. The world begins to noticeably pull back from the frantic pace associated with summer. This brings an invitation to look inward and reflect on what truly matters. This is the season of Metal Energy, a time to sharpen your focus, cut away the unnecessary and prepare yourself for the changes to come. Metal Energy is precise, clean and powerful in its simplicity. The energy of clarity and cutting through, it is the gleam of a polished blade and the stillness of a grey and empty sky. Following on from Earth energy's nurturing and holding, Metal energy now refines and resolves. Metal energy invites you to let go of what no longer serves you, to simplify your life in a way that is meaningful to you and to set your sight on the future with a renewed focus. Metal Energy relates to precision, simplification and refinement.

The Spirit of Metal energy

This is an energy that defines and distils, carving away the extraneous to reveal the essence of things. Just as the sculptor chisels the stone to uncover the form hidden within, so Metal energy invites liberation from excesses to reveal your own hidden form. Metal energy see what's missing or what's not working with an elegant ease of clarity. Lean into this energy to align with exactly what needs to be released.

Po is the Spirit of Metal energy the unconscious and instinctive Soul. The Po connects to your primal instincts, helping navigation through cycles of creation and destruction; life and death. Po understands the necessity of endings and the beauty of beginnings. In the Year of the Wood Snake Metal Energy mingles with the Snake's strategic wisdom, meaning this phase can be a powerful time for resolution and also preparation. As the year draws closer to its natural end Metal energy brings questions into sharp focus.

Ask yourself:

What do I need to release?

What truths must I address?

How can I refine my life to align with my values and priorities?

What would a simplified life look like for me?

As trees shed their leaves you are invited to let go of situations, habits, relationships and beliefs that no longer serve your Soul purpose. Simplifying your life is about creating space; Space for clarity, purpose and the things that truly matter to you. Simplifying life does not need to involve sacrifice, lean into the capacity of Metal energy to act as a detached observer and use discernment when cutting away any excess. This is the time to tie up loose ends, bring closure to unfinished business and to set a clear course for your future. Refine and streamline your goals and priorities to feel ready for the next phase to come.

Journal Prompts for Clarity, Simplicity and Letting Go

Letting Go:

What am I holding onto that no longer serves me? Why do I feel the need to hold on?

What would my life feel like if I let go of this burden / attachment?

How can I honour and release the parts of my past that are ready to fade?

What fears and insecurities am I ready to leave behind?

What old stories or beliefs about myself do I need to rewrite?

Simplifying Life:

What areas of my life feel cluttered or overwhelming? How can I simplify these?

What commitments or obligations do I currently have that no longer align with my values?

How can I create more physical, mental and emotional space in my life?

What do I want "living simply" to look like for me? How can I embrace and move toward this?

How can I bring more ease and flow into my daily routine?

Setting Priorities:

What truly matters to me? How can I prioritise it?

What are my top three values? How are these values reflected in my daily choices?

How can I align my time and energy with what's most important to me?

What distractions, habits, situations or relationships are pulling me away from my values, priorities and goals?

What loving boundaries do I need to set to honour myself and to protect my priorities?

Clarity for the Future:

What intentions do I want to carry forward into the next cycle?

What goals feel most meaningful to me right now?

What steps can I take to prepare for opportunities and challenges ahead?

How can I create a vision for my future that feels authentic and inspiring?

What lessons from this year can guide me in planning the year to come?

Looking Back to Look Ahead:

Taking a detached observers view of 2025 what am I most grateful for and what am I ready to leave behind?

Leverage Metal Energy for Refinement and Preparation

- **Conduct a Life Audit:** Review the different areas of your life; Values, Health, Spirituality, Creativity, Relationships, Career, Finances, Habits and Goals. Honestly identify what's working, what's not and what needs to change.
- **Streamline Your Commitments:** Simplify your schedule by letting go of obligations that no longer serve your purpose. Focus on quality rather than quantity.
- **Create Space for Clarity:** Dedicate time to stillness and loving detachment. Use tools such as meditation, journaling and quiet walks in nature to allow yourself space hear the inner voice that knows what's truly important.
- **Let Go with Ritual:** Release outdated attachments and unhelpful habits through intentional practices. Write a compassionate letter to a previous version of yourself, work with transformational painting, clay or collage to create a symbolic gesture of letting go.
- **Refine Your Goals:** Distil your intentions and plans into their essence. Focus on what truly resonates with you and set clear, actionable small steps for moving forward.

- **Prepare Your Environment:** Clear out physical clutter and create a space that reflects your values and supports your goals. How would you like your creative space to feel and look? What serves you best in your external environment to foster mental clarity and focus will be unique to you, create the environment that's right for you.
- **Celebrate Your Progress:** Acknowledge and honour how far you've travelled this year. Take time to appreciate your growth and transformation. Recognise your learning and notice where your growth edge now sits.

The Metal Energy of autumn is a powerful force for refinement and release. A time to let go of what no longer aligns with your path, to simplify your life and to prepare for the next cycle with clarity and intention. As you navigate through this phase embrace the sharpness of Metal energy's focus, its ability to cut away the unnecessary and its deep connection to resolution, simplification and clarity. Trust in the process of letting go, this is an inevitable loss however the grief of release is mitigated by the beauty of creating space for something new. This is your time to refine and resolve before stepping forward with renewed purpose and clarity.

Chapter 13
Creativity and the Five Elements: Inspiring the Artist, Innovator and Visionary Within

Creativity can feel like a single flame, however it is a constellation of sparks each ignited by the energies in and around you. The five elements; Water, Wood, Fire, Earth and Metal provide a powerful lens through which to explore and expand your creative practice. Whether you are a seasoned creative or a resistant beginner leaning into the unique energetic of each element can take your creativity to a whole new level. Each element moves with its own rhythm, has its own qualities and therefore provides artistic inspiration in different ways. Your own dominant energy shapes not only how you think, feel and act but also how you create.

Shaping your cycles of creativity.

In the Year of the Wood Snake, the Snake's wisdom, strategy and intuition is added into the mix guiding and shaping your cycles of creativity. Expanding your view of what creativity is and what the word means to you can generate room not only to embrace the hands on practical aspects of creating, also to acknowledge the energy of creativity in your own personal insight, transformation and growth. Each of the five energies can inspire a unique aspect of your creative process; from the quiet reflective stillness of Water to the fiery illuminating expression of Fire, each is just waiting for you to tap into it and experiment with the magic it can weave with your inner creative self.

This is your creative invitation to journey through the elements, exploring and experimenting with how each unique energy can awaken a new dimension of your creative self. Dive in and play with each element, integrate your journaling with artistic expression, problem-solving and innovation. Allow yourself to fully embrace the courage, freedom, fun, nourishment and clarity of deepening into your creativity as you flow through the year. You will find it utterly life enhancing and profoundly transformational.

Water: Creativity through Reflection and Seeing the Big Picture

Water is the birthplace of creativity, a space of stillness and introspection where ideas begin to quietly form. Holding the energy of intuition, hidden depths and an ability to leave its mark upon the world. The creativity of the Water phase can be silently profound with an ability to see the bigger picture and hold the stories of ancestry. Water energy creativity emerges from seemingly mysterious depths. Ensure your creative Water energy reserves and resources are constantly replenished by reading books, watching movies, plays and performances, listening to music, visiting galleries and surrounding yourself with artistic works and symbols that hold a special significance and meaning for you.

Inspiration

Water energy invites you to explore the unknown and dive into your inner world. What aspects of your creativity do you feel fearful of? What parts of your ancestry and your own story do you want to explore through creative practice? Trust this creative process of discovery, expand your perspective to see the bigger picture.

Practical Exercises for Earth Creativity:

Harvest Writing: Reflect on what you've created and achieved this year, then write about what you've learned and understood from the process.

- **Creative Cooking:** Prepare a meal as a creative act, focusing on colour, texture and flavour as forms of expression.
- **Gratitude Journal:** Write about the people, experiences and resources that have supported your creativity so far this year. Express gratitude for this support.
- **Clay Sculpting:** Get your hands in the earth! Work with clay or another tactile medium to create something simple and meaningful to you.
- **Root Drawing:** Draw or paint an image of a tree's roots; use this as a meditative practice to support you in understanding and integrating the foundations of your creativity.
- **Balance Mandala:** Create a mandala using natural objects or drawings that symbolise balance, harmony and late summer.
- **Creative Reflection:** Write a letter to yourself about your creative journey this year, celebrating your growth and resilience.

Metal: Creativity through Refinement and Focus

Metal is the energy of autumn; sharp and clear. This is the time to refine your work, focus on what matters and let go of what no longer serves your creative vision.

Inspiration

Metal encourages precision, clarity and the ability to release what is unnecessary

Practical Exercises for Metal Creativity:

- **Editing Session:** Revisit a creative project and refine it, focusing on clarity and impact. Editing is about change- what can you take away or add that will improve your project? This applies to all creative mediums; writing, art, music and more. Remember this is improvement in your eyes, what anyone else may think is irrelevant. Lean into Metal energy's ability to detach and let go to release any perfectionist tendencies.

- **Releasing Ritual:** Write a list of creative ideas or projects that you are ready to let go of. You may have outgrown these ideas or found a love and resonance in working with a different creative method or medium. It's okay to let go of unfinished projects and focus on what really matters to you now. Thank these projects for being part of your creative process and journey then cut up the list with scissors (symbolic of the ability of Metal energy to 'cut through') and dispose of the pieces.

- **Monochrome Art:** Create something using only one colour or medium, exploring its depth and nuance. Journal about what arises for you in this creative exercise.

- **Declutter Your Space:** Declutter and organise your creative workspace, removing anything that feels distracting or outdated.

- **Focus Journal:** Write about your top three creative priorities and how you plan to pursue them. What small steps could you take daily to move closer to completion of these projects?

- **Symbolic Sculpture:** Create a piece of art that represents clarity or letting go, using sharp or clean lines. Try fashioning your sculpture from aluminium/tin foil (kitchen foil) to symbolism Metal energy.

- **Completion Letter:** Metal energy loves to bring things to completion. Write a letter to your future-self dated one year from now. Outline the creative projects and goals you have completed in the year and the steps you took to achieve this. Give the letter to a trusted friend to post to you in one year's time.

A Year of Creativity with the Five Elements

Each phase of the Wood Snake year offers a unique opportunity to connect with the elements/ energies of the season and deepen your creative practice. By aligning with the energies of Water, Wood, Fire, Earth and Metal you can explore new dimensions of your artistry, innovation and problem-solving. Allow this journey through the elements to inspire you to create with intention, to embrace the cyclical nature of creativity and to trust the process of transformation. Just as the elements flow into one another, so too does your creative energy evolve, reflecting the world around you and the infinite potential within. Trust the energetic flow and trust your inner creative- you CAN be as creative as you dream to be.

Chapter 14
The Year of the Wood Snake: A Journey of Transformation and Growth

As you reach the conclusion of this book and the end of the year of the Wood Snake my hope is that you have experienced a profound, cyclical dance and a journey marked by growth, reflection, passion, grounding and clarity. Each season brought its own rhythm, each element its unique energy. Together weaving a tapestry of transformation that carried you from the still depths of winter to the sharp focus of autumn and back again to the edge of renewal. This year has not been about racing to a finish line or ticking off achievements. It has been about much something deeper; shedding old skins and letting go of that which you have outgrown. Embracing your creative spark within and moving forward with intention and purpose. Now, as the year winds down, it's time to reflect on how far you've come, what you've learned and how you've grown.

A Recap of the Journey

Winter (Water Energy): Rest, Reflection and Intuition: The year began in stillness with the quiet contemplative energy of Water. This phase invited you to slow down, to listen deeply to the currents of your soul and to plant the seeds of your intentions. It was a time to dream, to release fears and to honour the wisdom that arises in silence.

Spring (Wood Energy): Growth, Creativity and Expansion: Spring brought the vitality of Wood, a season of bold beginnings and fresh potential. This was a time for setting intentions, exploring your creativity and stepping into the expansive energy of growth. The world opened up and so did you; stretching toward new horizons with curiosity and courage.

Summer (Fire Energy): Passion, Expression and Joy: In summer, Fire ignited your passions and brought your creativity to life. This was the season of connection, of sharing your light with the world and of daring to express your authentic self. It reminded you to embrace the moment, to celebrate the joy of simply being alive and to let your inner flame burn brightly.

Late Summer (Earth Energy): Grounding, Stability and Gratitude: Late summer brought balance and stability, a time to pause and appreciate the fruits of your labour. The Earth element offered grounding, helping you consolidate your progress and integrate your experiences. It was a season to reflect on what nourishes you and to honour the relationships and values that hold you steady.

Autumn (Metal Energy): Clarity, Simplification and Resolution: The final phase, guided by Metal, was one of refinement and letting go. Autumn called you to release what no longer served you, to simplify your life and to sharpen your focus. It was a season of preparation, of setting your priorities and of finding clarity as you looked ahead to the next cycle.

Revisiting Your Journey

The gifts contained within the Year of the Yin Wood Snake don't end here. The lessons, insights, creative sparks, growth and transformation you have gathered and experienced through this year are yours to carry forward. Before you leap into the next chapter, gift yourself some time to revisit the pages of your journal, the projects you started and the intentions you set.

Revisit Your Journal Entries:

Look back on your thoughts, reflections and dreams from the past year. Be kind, loving and compassionate with yourself as you reread your journal. This is NOT an invitation to beat yourself up, this is an opportunity to honestly and loving reflect and observe.

Ask yourself:

What patterns or themes are emerging throughout my journal?

What insights feel especially meaningful to me now?

Highlight the moments that resonate most, allow these to guide you as you move forward.

Reflect on Creative Projects:

Whether you completed your projects or they remain works in progress, revisit your creative endeavours with fresh eyes. Be kind, loving and compassionate with yourself as your revisit your creative ventures. This is NOT an invitation to beat yourself up, this is an opportunity to honestly and lovingly reflect and observe.

Ask Yourself:

What did I learn about myself through the process?

How can these projects inspire and guide my next steps?

Celebrate Your Growth

Take a moment to honour how far you've come. Growth isn't always easy or linear. However each step, no matter how small, has brought you closer to your true authentic self and that is worth celebrating.

Moving Forward with the Wisdom of the Wood Snake

As you prepare to step into a new year, carry the wisdom of the Wood Snake with you. Hold onto the quiet strength, intuitive wisdom and ability to shed what you have outgrown. Trust that your transformation is an ongoing process, one that unfolds in cycles, just like the seasons.

Guiding principles to carry you forward

- **Stay Rooted in Your Values:** Let your values be the foundation of your actions and decisions. They are your compass in times of uncertainty.

- **Embrace Creativity as a Practice:** Creativity isn't just something you do, it is a way of being. Continue to explore, experiment, PLAY and express yourself without fear of judgement.

- **Honour Both Movement and Stillness:** Growth happens in states of both action and rest. Give yourself permission to ebb and flow with the rhythms of life.

- **Trust the Process:** Transformation takes time. Trust in your journey, even when the path ahead seems unclear.

A Closing Reflection

Reaching a destination was not the aim of the Year of the Yin Wood Snake. It has been about the journey of navigating the twists and turns with curiosity, grace and courage. About finding beauty in the process, meaning in the challenges and joy in the moments of connection and creation. As this year comes to a close, know that you are not the same person who began it. You've grown, shed old skins and discovered new facets of yourself. And as you stand on the threshold of the next cycle, carry this truth with you: You are a work in progress, endlessly evolving, endlessly creating. And most importantly YOU ARE ENOUGH, YOU HAVE ALWAYS BEEN ENOUGH.

Take a loving deep breath: Feel the energy of the Wood Snake settling within you, a quiet steady strength that will guide you wherever you go.

Your journey isn't over...

It's just beginning.

Chapter 15
Onward to the Year of the Fire Horse: A Year of Bold Momentum

As the final embers of the Wood Snake year glow and fade, the horizon ahead blazes with a fiery energy. 2026 brings the Year of the Yang Fire Horse, a year that promises to be electrifying and FAST! Where the Wood Snake guided us through a journey of transformation, introspection and deliberate growth, the Fire Horse will charge in with unbridled energy, daring us to leap boldly into action.

The Horse is a creature of freedom, passion, unstoppable movement and so much more. When combined with the Yang Fire element, its energy becomes a force of nature; dynamic, vibrant and, at times, intense. This year of the Yin Wood Snake year has taught you to trust the process and embrace transformation, in 2026 the Fire Horse year will challenge you to act, to take risks and to ignite your boldest dreams into reality.

A Glimpse of the Year Ahead

The Year of the Fire Horse is not for the faint of heart. Its Yang energy is outward, assertive and demanding, the energy of Fire brings heat, illumination and the spark of creativity. Together, they create a year of momentum and opportunity. 2026 will also require you to focus, balance and be selective to avoid burnout.

The Snake has moved with precision and strategy, be ready for the Horse to gallop ahead with enthusiasm and daring. 2026 will be a year to pursue passions, to take decisive action and to embrace the power of possibility. The Horse can be impulsive and the Fire Horse year will also ask you to harness this energy with intention, ensuring that your actions align with your values and goals.

What to Expect in the Fire Horse Year:

- **High-Energy Movement:** The Fire Horse thrives on action. 2026 will be a year for tackling big projects, launching new ventures and pushing past limitations.

- **Creativity on Fire:** Fire energy fuels bold, passionate creativity. In the Yang year of the Fire Horse let your imagination run wild and embrace innovation in all its forms.

- **Risk and Reward:** The Horse will encourage you to take risks, however it's essential to weigh those risks with clarity and the illumination that Fire energy offers. Balance impulsiveness with wisdom in 2026.

- **Freedom and Exploration:** The Horse craves independence and adventure. 2026 will be a year to break free from constraints and explore new horizons, both literal and metaphorical.

- **Challenges of Focus:** With so much energy in the air staying grounded and focused will be key. The lessons of the Wood Snake year; patience, strategic wisdom and reflection will serve as a valuable anchor as you move into 2026.

The Year of the Yang Fire Horse:

Watch out for my essential guide to the energies of The Year of the Yang Fire Horse:

Galloping Through Fire: Journaling for Passion, Action and Creative Freedom in 2026

(Published by Spiritual Bookworm)

This new book will be your guide to harnessing the fiery energy of 2026 with focus, creativity and purpose. From monthly themes to journal prompts, rituals and creative practices, it will offer tools to help you navigate the excitement and challenges of this bold and transformative year.

Alongside this crucial book I will once again be facilitating the 'Creative Journal Quest' for 2026 for those who yearn to join an online community of like-minded Souls. Join the waitlist for the next book launch and enrolment for the Creative Journal Quest: 2026 at www.debconnor.com

Final Thoughts

The Year of the Wood Snake has given you the wisdom of transformation, the grace of letting go and the courage to grow. As you prepare to step into the dynamic energy of the Fire Horse year, remember that you are carrying your transformation, growth and learning from 2025 with you. This wisdom is your compass and foundation; a steady quiet strength amidst the whirlwind ahead. The Fire Horse will gallop into your life, inviting you to move, create and live boldly. Allow it inspire you to follow your passions, to take risks that set your soul on fire and to embrace the freedom to be unapologetically YOU. Your journey is (once again) only just beginning. I look forward to connecting with you again in 2026; ready to gallop into the flames of creativity, courage and adventure.

Stay aligned; stay curious;
let your Spirit shine brightly!

Chapter 16
Month by Month Overview: Themes, Energies, and Suggested Practices

The energetics of the Year of the Yin Wood Snake shift and change throughout 2025. Each month has its own rhythm, influenced by the elemental phase and the sway of the Wood Snake. This month by month guide to navigating the year invites you to explore a unique monthly theme rooted in the energy of the season. Your invitation to deeper alignment and harmony with the energetic phase is offered through suggested practices including meditations*, rituals, creative pursuits, and body movement practices to support you in connecting with the element and Spirit of each month.

January: A Month of Deep Stillness (Water Energy)

Theme: Rest and Introspection

January invites you into the quiet depths of Water Energy, a time to reflect, restore and gather your inner strength. This is the space between the exhale of the old year and the inhale of the new.

- **Meditative Practice:** Guided visualization of a frozen lake, exploring what lies beneath the surface.*
- **Ritual:** Write a letter to yourself reflecting on the past year, (2024: the year of the Yang Wood Dragon), remind yourself of your level of resources and reserves at the turn of the year. Seal your letter in an envelope, store your letter as a symbol of storing resources. Leave your letter unopened until next January (2026: the year of the Fire Horse) when you can lovingly review your words with compassion and thoughtfulness.
- **Creative Pursuit:** Create a vision board that reflects your ideal year ahead. Focus on the feelings you want to experience and the energies you want to align to rather than specific goals (they can come later in the Wood energy phase). Use minimal words and maximum symbolic imagery, utilising colours and textures to express yourself.
- **Body Movement Practice:** Gentle yin yoga or restorative stretching to honour your need for resting and recharging.

February: A Month of Quiet Awakening (Water Energy)

Theme: Renewal and Inner Listening

With winter still in its depths, February invites you to tune into your intuition and begin setting quiet intentions for the year.

- **Meditative Practice:** Quiet breath focused meditation; allowing intuitive guidance to emerge*.
- **Ritual:** Cleanse your living space with sage or incense, symbolically thanking and saying goodbye to the lingering energies of the Yang Wood Dragon Year.
- **Creative Pursuit:** Begin collecting a resource of inspirations: Dedicate a journal to an assemblage of quotes, sketches, photographs and ideas that feed your inner creative reservoir.
- **Body Movement Practice:** Practice slow tai chi or qigong to cultivate flow and inner harmony.

March: A Month of Emerging Growth (Wood Energy)

Theme: Planting Seeds of Intention

Spring begins with the stirring energy of Wood, inviting you to take your first steps toward growth and creation.

- **Meditative Practice:** Guided visualization meditation of seed planting, growth and connection with your imagination and intentions.*
- **Ritual:** Write down your dreams, intentions and goals for the year using non-toxic ink and biodegradable paper and bury these beside a growing tree (being careful not to damage any delicate tree roots).
- **Creative Pursuit:** Sketch, paint, collage and/or write poetry about the dreams you want to nurture and grow during this year. Give them a creative form that is meaningful to you, let your imagination run free. Remember this is for you, no one else, therefore it only needs to make sense and resonate with you.
- **Body Movement Practice:** Dynamic vinyasa yoga or brisk walking to align with the burgeoning Wood energy and inspire action.

April: A Month of Fresh Potential (Wood Energy)

Theme: Creativity in Bloom

The energy of April brings vitality and new imaginative ideas. Wood energy continues to encourage exploration and bold creativity.

- **Meditative Practice:** Guided meditation on embracing the creative nature of curiosity.*
- **Ritual:** Create a collage of intentions; fill a display board with photographs, sketches, drawings, paintings, symbols and notes which represent your creative goals.
- **Creative Pursuit:** Experiment with a creative medium that is new to you. Keep your explorations playful, allowing yourself freedom to create without boundaries or expectations.
- **Body Movement Practice:** Dance freely to music that calls you. Practice Five Rhythms Dance and allow your body to express itself intuitively.

May: A Month of Growing Confidence (Wood Energy)

Theme: Nurturing Growth

In May Wood energy invites you to tend to your goals with care and persistence. A time to plan ahead and to dream BIG in your visions.

- **Meditative Practice:** Guided meditation for visioning and planning for your dreams and embodying gratitude for the growth you've experienced so far.*
- **Ritual:** Enjoy time in nature, plant flowers, herbs and/or trees as a metaphor for your continued growth.
- **Creative Pursuit:** Write a short story or poem inspired by themes of growth, creativity and imagination.
- **Body Movement Practice:** Strength-building exercises to embody a feeling of steady progress. Mobility and flexibility exercises to counter the tendency of Wood energy to stagnate.

June: A Month of Radiance (Fire Energy)

Theme: Joy and Connection

June welcomes in the warmth of Fire Energy, a season for passion, connections and wholehearted living.

- **Meditative Practice:** Guided meditation to discover the hidden jewels and connections to be found when entering the back of the Heart.*
- **Ritual:** Host a gathering or celebration to share your joy and gratitude with loved ones.
- **Creative Pursuit:** Foster connections by embracing a collaborative project, invite others to contribute to a creative project.
- **Body Movement Practice:** Ecstatic dance to channel energy, release inhibitions and embrace the joy of movement. If Fire energy feels overly exuberant dipping into Water energy and swimming can quell the overactive Fire.

July: A Month of Bold Action (Fire Energy)

Theme: Expressing Passion

With summer in full swing July invites you to take bold action toward your dreams and let your light shine brightly.

- **Meditative Practice:** Guided meditative visualization of your most vibrant self; opening to living your passions fully.*
- **Ritual:** Light a candle to symbolise radiating your own brightness. Acknowledge where in your life you need to shine your light, what areas of your life would benefit from honest heartfelt illumination? Voice your acknowledgements aloud and set your intentions to move forward with Self-Love.
- **Creative Pursuit:** Begin a project that scares you... in a good way! Push your artistic boundaries creating in a medium you love.
- **Body Movement Practice:** Lean into the connection of Fire energy by engaging with a group activity; join a group for Qi Gong or go hiking with a group to connect with nature and others.

August: A Month of Nourishment (Earth Energy)

Theme: Celebrating Abundance

As summer softens into late summer towards the end of August grounding energy emerges inviting you to celebrate what you've achieved.

- **Meditative Practice:** Guided meditation, focusing on feeling the sensations of nourishment and contentment in the body, allowing overthinking to subside.*
- **Ritual:** In the spirit of harvest and the nourishment of Earth energy, prepare a meal with seasonal produce, savour the process and the flavours. Invite loved ones to share a collective meal as a sacred ritual in honour of the ability of Earth energy to create community.
- **Creative Pursuit:** Create an altar using seasonal found items, from nature and things from your home environment, include your own hand written notes and sketches that resonate with Earth energy's giving nature.
- **Body Movement Practice:** Engage with gentle Pilates or restorative yoga to nourish your physicality and align with your body's rhythms.

September: A Month of Integration & Assimilation (Earth Energy)

Theme: Finding Balance

September's energy invites you to integrate your experiences and find a grounding stability before moving forward.

- **Meditative Practice:** Guided meditation for integration and assimilation focusing on calming overthinking and being present.*
- **Ritual:** Stand barefoot on the Earth and feel her grounding and support, recite a poem or prayer aloud in honour of your connection to the Earth.
- **Creative Pursuit:** Design a mandala which symbolises your personal journey of growth, understanding and integration. Get your hands in some clay and 'create what is to use what is not' by crafting a small thumb pot.
- **Body Movement Practice:** Grounding practices such as standing Qi Gong and gentle walks in nature.

October: A Month of Refinement (Metal Energy)

Theme: Letting Go

As autumn deepens, October invites you to release what no longer serves you and creating space for clarity.

- **Meditative Practice:** Guided meditation on letting go, visualising any perceived burdens falling away like leaves.*
- **Ritual:** Write down what you want to release and let go of then cut up your list into smaller parts, imagining the sharp clarity of Metal energy cutting through and aiding your release. Drop the pieces into a fire as you recite a poem or prayer about letting go aloud.
- **Creative Pursuit:** Create a piece of abstract art inspired by the theme of shedding an old skin, letting go and releasing. Incorporate metallic paints and metal leaf into your artwork to symbolise the presence of Metal energy.
- **Body Movement Practice:** Practice light, repetitive movements such as walking, Tai Chi or Qi Gong to encourage flow. With your movements imagine letting go and releasing that which no longer serves you.

November: A Month of Clarity (Metal Energy)

Theme: Simplifying and Focusing

November brings a sharp clarity and an invitation to simplify your life, streamline your priorities and focus on what matters most to you.

- **Meditative Practice:** Guided meditation for mental clarity, inviting simplification and attaining the focus of a detached observer using breathwork.*
- **Ritual:** Declutter a space in your home; Engage with the decluttering process as sacred practice and clear and clean your space with gratitude and reverence. As you declutter repeat the mantra "the more I clear the more clarity and focus I have".
- **Creative Pursuit:** Write a list of your core values and explore how they shape your creativity. Do particular values lend themselves to particular artistic mediums? Play and experiment with creating with one of your values as a theme.
- **Body Movement Practice:** Engage with strength-focused exercises to embody focus and determination. Try kettlebells or similar remembering to focus on breathing while exercising.

December: A Month of Resolution (Metal / Water Energy)

Theme: Preparing for Renewal

The year ends with the beautiful stillness of Metal Energy sliding into the Water Energy phase, a time to resolve, reflect, and prepare for the new cycle to come.

- **Meditative Practice:** Guided meditation focusing on your inner light and bringing calm and stillness to the mind.*
- **Ritual:** Write a letter to the year ahead; 2026, the Year of the Yang Fire Horse, include your hopes, dreams and intentions. Add any questions or special requests you have for the approaching 'Fire Horse' into your letter. Ask how the Horse might carry you where you need to go. Seal your letter in an envelope and address it to yourself, give your sealed letter to a trusted friend and ask them to mail it to you when they feel the time is right.
- **Creative Pursuit:** Compile a visual art journal reflecting on the Year of the Wood-Snake, include images that symbolise your growth and transformation. Create a visual celebration of yourself.
- **Body Movement Practice:** Work with gentle movements such as Tai Chi, Qi Gong or Yin yoga to embrace stillness.

Living the Year with Intention

The Year of the Wood Snake is inviting you into a 12 month cycle of deep transformation, each phase building on the last, each energy guiding you toward growth, harmony and rebirth. Align yourself each month with the prevailing energetic, engage with practices which harmonise with these rhythms to navigate your year with clarity, creativity and purpose. Embrace the wisdom of the Wood Snake, trust your inner knowing. Lean into the Snake's strategic intention and precise action to weave a year that is uniquely and profoundly yours.

*Guided audio meditations are available FREE to participants on the online 'Creative Journal Quest: 2025' with Rev Deb. If you are not a participant and would like purchase the downloadable audio meditations please email: deb@debconnor.com

An Invitation to Continue your Journey: Expanding Your Creative Horizons

Your journey through the Year of the Wood Snake has been one of depth, transformation and growth. I promise it has, even if that's not how it has felt, even if you feel you didn't make as much progress as you wanted to. You are not the same version of yourself that began this journey at the start of the Year of the Yin Wood Snake. It has been my honour and privilege to guide you through this year, offering tools, reflections, prompts, creative practices and rituals to awaken your inner wisdom and creativity. And the journey doesn't have to end here. If you feel something awakening within you; a desire to go deeper, to awaken your creative spirit, to connect more fully with your purpose and your true authentic self, or if you crave community and connection with like-minded Souls I invite you to join me in exploring these pathways further. Whether you're looking to deepen your journaling practice, find new sources of creative inspiration, or immerse yourself in a community of fellow seekers there are many ways we can work together.

Visit www.debconnor.com to join the waiting list for courses, workshops, group or individual coaching.

Arts for Awakening

A transformative exploration of art as a gateway to self-discovery and spiritual growth. This online course will guide you in using creative practices to awaken your intuition, connect with your authentic self and express your soul's truth.

The Sacred Journal Quest

Take your journaling practice to the next level with this deeply immersive course. Explore journaling as a sacred act, one that unlocks your inner wisdom, reveals hidden truths and helps you navigate life with clarity and purpose.

Find Your Creative Inspiration

Are you feeling creatively blocked or uninspired? This self-paced online course is a spark for your imagination, offering tools, exercises and prompts to reignite your creative fire and help you see the world with fresh eyes.

The Creative Spiritual Quest: A 3-Month Online Mastermind

Embark on a transformative 3-month journey with a small group of like-minded souls. The Creative Spiritual Quest is an intimate online mastermind designed to nurture your creative spirit while deepening your connection to yourself and your purpose. Together, we'll explore the intersection of creativity and spirituality, using guided practices, group coaching and shared experience as inspiration to unlock new possibilities in your life and work. This is a space for profound growth, meaningful connection, and the kind of transformation that only happens when you journey with others who share your passion and curiosity.

Individual Coaching (Limited availability: apply online to join the waitlist)

For those who are ready to really take their creativity and their life to the next level. You'll need to be serious about investing in yourself and your creative practice. Individualised creativity coaching offers a bespoke experience tailored to your unique energies, journey and creative desires. If you are committed to starting or completing your project, overcoming your creative blocks and aligning your creative work with your deeper purpose, I work with you on a Soul level to unlock your fullest potential, supporting you to create a life infused with meaning, inspiration and creativity.

Why Work With Me?

I believe creativity is a sacred act, a way of connecting with your essence and bringing it into the world. I'm passionate about helping you discover the richness of your creative spirit, the clarity of your inner voice and the joy that comes from expressing your authentic self.

Take that Step: Your Creative Soul is calling you forward

If you feel the pull to continue your journey and uncover your own creative way, I invite you to reach out; explore my offerings to discover the path that resonates most deeply with you. I'm here to guide and support you as you step boldly into your creative power.

Harness your momentum:
Let's create, explore and grow together.

About the Author

Rev. Deb Connor (Monk Li Xiào Yì 笑意) is a writer, abstract artist, interfaith minister and 22nd-generation Dragon Gate Daoist Monk. She weaves creativity, spirituality and ancient wisdom into transformative journeys for the Soul. A Visual Medicine facilitator and journal therapist, she uses creative practice to help individuals and groups explore growth, spirituality and self-discovery.

A former NHS clinical educator turned creative spiritual guide, Rev. Deb has invested decades supporting others' evolution through her online programmes and her acupuncture clinic, Acupuncture Care, in St Helens, Merseyside.

She shares her insightful reflections on creativity, spirituality and the Daoist path through her popular Substack Creative Spirit with Rev Deb. A sought-after conference speaker, she is known for her fun and inspiring talks on spirituality, creativity and personal transformation. Her previous books The Little Book of Dao and The 12 Step Colouring Book have inspired many on their growth journey.

In Embracing the Wisdom of the Wood Snake: Shedding, Growing and Journaling through 2025, Rev. Deb draws on her experience as a journal therapist, her deep connection to nature and Daoist five element philosophy to guide you through a year of transformation.

When she isn't writing or mentoring others you'll find her immersed in abstract painting, renovating a grade II listed chapel on Anglesey with husband Neil, or out walking with her beloved greyhounds.

Also by Rev. Deb Connor

The Little Book of Dao:

One liners of wisdom inspired by the Daodejing

'The Little Book of Dao' and the accompanying companion journal and doodle pad books are inspired by Rev Deb's love of the classic Daoist text the DaoDeJing. Rev Deb distilled and lovingly fermented the words of her Daoist teachers and study of various translations of the DaoDeJing in her often overactive mind for many years before 'accidentally' writing 'The Little Book of Dao'.

The Little Book of Dao

Companion Doodle Pad

'The Little Book of Dao' and the accompanying companion journal and doodle pad books are inspired by Rev Deb's love of the classic Daoist text the DaoDeJing. Rev Deb distilled and lovingly fermented the words of her Daoist teachers and study of various translations of the DaoDeJing in her often overactive mind for many years before 'accidentally' writing 'The Little Book of Dao'.

The 12 Step Colouring Book

The 12 step colouring book is over 100 pages of colouring fun! Scribble, draw, paint And colour your way through the 12 steps of recovery.

Printed in Great Britain
by Amazon

59108319R00185